The AWESOME OFFICIAL Guide to

Disney

CLUB PENGUIN ™

EXPANDED EDITION

D0291682

by Katherine Noll and Tracey West

Grosset & Dunlap
An Imprint of Penguin Group (USA) Inc.

GROSSET & DUNLAP
Published by the Penguin Group
Penguin Group (USA) Inc., 375 Hudson Street,
New York, New York 10014, USA
Penguin Group (Canada), 90 Eglinton Avenue East, Suite 700,
Toronto, Ontario M4P 2Y3, Canada
(a division of Pearson Penguin Canada Inc.)
Penguin Books Ltd., 80 Strand, London WC2R ORL, England
Penguin Group Ireland, 25 St. Stephen's Green, Dublin 2, Ireland
(a division of Penguin Books Ltd.)
Penguin Group (Australia), 250 Camberwell Road,
Camberwell, Victoria 3124, Australia
(a division of Pearson Australia Group Pty. Ltd.)
Penguin Books India Pvt. Ltd., 11 Community Centre,
Panchsheel Park, New Delhi–110 017, India
Penguin Group (NZ), 67 Apollo Drive, Rosedale,
North Shore 0632, New Zealand
(a division of Pearson New Zealand Ltd.)
Penguin Books (South Africa) (Pty.) Ltd., 24 Sturdee Avenue,
Rosebank, Johannesburg 2196, South Africa

Penguin Books Ltd., Registered Offices:
80 Strand, London WC2R ORL, England

Library of Congress Control Number: 2010005979

ISBN 978-0-448-45395-8   10 9 8 7 6 5 4 3 2 1

Hey, You! Yes, You!

We've seen that look on your face before. It's a mix of excitement and anticipation. With all the fun things to do on Club Penguin, where do you begin? Between exploring the island, meeting new friends, playing games, and going to parties, there's always something new to do. The action on Club Penguin changes faster than a penguin sliding down an icy slope in *Sled Racing*! In fact, so much has changed since *The Ultimate Official Guide to Club Penguin: Volume 1* came out, that a new edition had to be written to keep track of it all.

All this exciting new stuff can make your head spin. Well, tell your head it's time to stop spinning! You're on your way to becoming a Club Penguin expert by reading this guidebook.

This book is filled with all the tips, secrets, and facts you'll need to make your way around Club Penguin like a real pro. Before long you'll be holding parties in your igloo and serving pizzas at the Pizza Parlor.

We've said enough. Now it's your turn. Check out what's on these pages, and when you're done, log in to Club Penguin and let us know what you think. We always love to hear what you have to say!

Your friends,
The Club Penguin Team

Table of Contents

Mini-Games:

Getting Started

Look for These Penguins as You Read

Hello, dear reader! As editor in chief of *The Club Penguin Times*, I receive an extraordinary number of questions from penguins every day. I'll make your journey through this book easier by sharing my favorite facts, tips, and secrets.

I'm a Club Penguin Tour Guide. I'll be introducing you to the different sections of this book—and different areas of Club Penguin.

Internet Safety First

- **Always keep personal information to yourself.** Never share it online! That includes your real name, age, address, location, phone number, or school.

- **Always keep your password safe and private.** Never share it with anyone but your parent or guardian. If someone else gets it, they might pretend to be you, give out personal information, or get you into trouble.

- **Tell a parent if someone says or does something on the Internet that makes you feel uncomfortable.** Also tell them if someone asks you for personal information.

- **Only visit sites on the Internet that are monitored by moderators.** On Club Penguin, moderators are highly trained members of the staff who monitor behavior and chat. If a penguin says or does something inappropriate, you can report them to a moderator. Click the penguin, and their player card will appear. Choose the Ⓜ to make a report.

Club Penguin Rules

1. Always have fun!

2. Safety first. Do not ask another penguin for personal information such as their real name or phone number.

3. Use appropriate language. Do not swear or use other bad language.

4. Always help other penguins who ask for your help.

5. Respect other penguins. Do not act in any way that is mean or rude.

6. Do not ask anyone for their password.

If you break any of the rules, you risk being banned from Club Penguin by one of our moderators on staff. This means you will not be able to use your account for a period of time. Sometimes it's for twenty-four hours, or it could be forever. Remember that another player cannot ban you from the site—only a moderator can.

Creating Your Penguin

Many penguins visit Club Penguin every day, but each one is as unique as a snowflake. One of the best things about being a penguin is that you can be whomever you want to be. Here are some things to think about as you create your penguin personality:

- Choose your favorite color to start—then add more colors as you play. You can change colors to match your mood or favorite clothing combo.

- Choose a background for your player card that reflects your interests.

- Use actions like dancing or throwing a snowball to show off your playful side.

- Express your friendly nature by helping other penguins in need.

- Experiment! If you try something and don't like it, just give something else a try.

Your Name

Choosing the right name is important. Once you choose your penguin name, it's yours forever! If a friend asks you for help in choosing a name, try these suggestions:

1. **Never use your real name!** That's a basic rule for Internet safety.

2. **Use your imagination.** Try a made-up name. One penguin we know is named I 8 A B, for example.

3. **Think of your favorite things.** Your favorite animal or sports team could be part of your name.

4. **Add some numbers.** If the name you want is taken, add some numbers to it to make it different. For example: DaisyGirl910. For safety reasons, don't use your birthday or address.

5. **Remember:** Make sure your name is between four and twelve characters long. Once you come up with your name, write it down along with your password. Give this to a parent or guardian and ask them to keep it safe for you, in case you forget.

Check Out the Home Page

Be sure to explore the home page at clubpenguin.com before you dive in and play. There are a lot of helpful features to check out on the website before you get in the game.

Click on the word *Community* to find the What's New blog. It's a quick way to find out about upcoming parties, special events, new games, and everything else that's happening on the island.

Click on the blue penguin to see video that shows what Club Penguin has to offer.

Click on the penguins on the bottom of the screen to download coloring pages, learn about membership, get help, and more.

Fun Stuff

Submit your artwork, get new desktop wallpapers, coloring pages and the latest comics.

Check It Out

When I visit the home page, I enjoy clicking on the different items I see there, such as the blue phone. Try it and see what happens!

AUNT ARCTIC SAYS

Membership   Community   Parents   Shop   Help

FEATURES LAUNCHED!!

PLAY NOW!

embership
arn about the features
l benefits of becoming
member of Club
nguin.

arn more

Online Shop
Take Club Penguin with
you. Check out the shop
to see the latest in
penguin gear.

Go Shopping

Help & Support
Find answers to the most
frequent questions about
Club Penguin. Updated
weekly.

Get Help

Parents
Learn more about Club
Penguin in this section
designed for parents of
penguins.

Learn more

Using Your Toolbar

Once you log in, it's helpful to know how to use your toolbar.

 Speech Bubble: Click here to see a list of pre-written comments. Click on any of the comments and the words will appear in a speech bubble over your head. It's a quick way to say "hi" or ask a question, such as, "Where did you find that pin?"

 Winking Face: Click here for a list of emotes—little icons that show how you're feeling without using words.

 Blue Penguin: Click here for a list of motions you can make: dance, wave, or sit.

 Snowball: Click on the snowball to throw a snowball. A round circle will appear on your screen after you click. Move the circle to the place you want your snowball to land. Then click.

Speech Bar: Use this bar to type in your own messages if you are not in Ultimate Safe Chat. When you are done typing, press the speech bubble to the right of the bar. The message will appear in a bubble over your head.

Badge: If you are a member, click on the badge to bring your player card up on the screen.

 Star: If you are not a member, you can click on the star instead of the badge to bring up your player card.

 Smiley Face: Click on this to see a list of your buddies. You can click on a buddy's name at any time to see their player card. If a buddy is online, you will see a yellow face next to your buddy's name.

 House: Click on this to enter your igloo.

 Question Mark: Click on the question mark to get to your account settings. You can change your password, cancel your membership, or activate Ultimate Safe Chat. You can also find out how old your penguin is.

Do More with a Membership

It doesn't cost any money to join Club Penguin. But a parent or guardian can sign you up for a membership and pay a monthly fee. A membership allows you to do more on Club Penguin.

Create More: Purchase clothing, decorate your igloo, and discover special actions that your penguin can do.

Explore More: Access more levels in games and explore new areas first.

Play More: Adopt as many as sixteen puffles.

Access More: Get backstage passes at parties.

Celebrate More: Attend members-only parties and events.

You're In! What Now?

Waddle Around. Use your mouse to move your penguin and follow the paths to different areas of Club Penguin.

Get Room Tips. Discover tips in every room by using your mouse to roll over the area. These tips will help you get to know what you can do in each room and where you can go.

Use the Map. Click on the 🗺️ on the lower left of your screen. Then click on where you want to go.

Find Your Igloo. Click on the 🏠 in the toolbar if you want to chill out in your igloo.

Get the News. Check out *The Club Penguin Times* by clicking on the 📰 on the top left of your screen. You can also read the Notice Board (which you can access from the 🗺️ or your igloo) to find out what's happening around the island.

Take a Tour. Ask a Tour Guide to show you around so you don't have to explore solo.

Coming soon—the next time you log in to Club Penguin, you just might find yourself in a new location, where you'll be able to get the latest news, learn more about your favorite games and rooms, and find a Tour Guide. Here are just some of the things you'll find there:

Notice Board: Find out which penguins are throwing igloo parties or looking for band members, for example.

Tour Guide Booth: Instead of going to the Ski Village, you can find a Tour Guide or take the Tour Guide test here.

Fish Fountain: This cool new addition to the island will spout water out of a golden fish's mouth!

Take a Tour, Give a Tour

Before 2007: New penguins waddled around the island. They got lost and didn't know who to ask for help.

After 2007: Friendly Tour Guides appeared to show newcomers around, making their experience better with facts, game tips, and advice.

Today: You can take a tour by approaching a Tour Guide and asking for one. Click on 💬 (or look under Questions if you are in Ultimate Safe Chat mode). You can also apply to be a Tour Guide yourself when your penguin is forty-five days old.

Being a Tour Guide is a wonderful way to help other penguins. Go to the Tour Guide Booth and click on the sign. If you are old enough, you will be asked to take a quiz. If you pass, you will earn your official Tour Guide hat. You can find it by clicking on the clothing tab on your player card.

AUNT ARCTIC SAYS

Five Reasons to Become a Tour Guide

1. It's a great way to make new friends.

2. Helping other penguins can give you a warm feeling on a chilly day.

3. New penguins will be impressed with your knowledge of "secret" facts and places.

4. The Tour Guide script makes it super easy. Just click on  and go to "Activities." Then "Give a tour."

5. You get to wear a cool hat!

If you're touring the Lighthouse, see if you can spot a model Snow Trekker on the back wall!

HINT

TOURS

Tour Guide Study Guide

Before you can earn your Tour Guide hat, you need to take a quiz. If you answer each question correctly, you can begin giving tours right away.

Does the word *quiz* make you break out into a cold sweat? Don't worry! Follow these tips and you'll speed through the questions faster than a penguin sliding over a patch of ice!

Visit every room you can. A good Tour Guide has something to say about every place on the island. You may know every inch of the Pizza Parlor by heart, but before you take the quiz, make sure you visit spots you don't go to that often. Make a note of what the room looks like and what happens there.

Play every game. You need to be familiar with the games to pass the quiz, so make sure you've played each one at least once. See, studying can be fun!

Adopt a puffle. Play with your puffle, feed it, and take care of it. As a Tour Guide, you can pass along your puffle knowledge to other penguins.

Explore the catalogs. Even if you don't have a membership, there are items in the catalogs you can buy. Become familiar with these items, and make sure to look for hidden items in the catalogs as well. Roll your cursor over objects and words. If a hand symbol pops up, click on it to reveal the hidden item.

Congratulations!
on becoming a tour guide!

Learn secrets: A new secret is revealed in every issue of the newspaper. You can also find lots of secrets in the pages of this book!

Town Center

There's always something happening in the Town Center. It's home to the Coffee Shop, the Night Club, and the Gift Shop. So whether you're in the mood to curl up with a good book and cocoa at the Coffee Shop, dance the day away at the Night Club, or shop for something new to wear, you can do it all right here.

The Town Center is also a great place to penguin-watch. Take a seat in front of the Coffee Shop and see who passes by. If you see penguins having a snowball fight or playing tag, join in!

Kick Back in the Coffee Shop

The minute you walk inside, you hear the strains of a reggae beat, setting a funky vibe for this room. Take a seat on one of the comfy red couches. You may see a server in an apron working, ready to pour you a hot, tasty beverage. Drink a cup while you read the newspaper, chat with friends, or meet new penguins.

If you're looking to earn extra coins, waddle over to the bags of java and play *Bean Counters*. If you're the type of penguin who is interested in the arts, head upstairs to the Book Room.

HINT

If you like the service your penguin waiter has given you, don't forget to leave a tip. Press the E and M keys on your keyboard at the same time and a coin symbol will appear.

We are very lucky that our island is filled with penguins who want to help out! If you, too, would like to serve coffee at the Coffee Shop, you'll need to get the green apron. From time to time, it can be found for sale in the Gift Shop. To perform the pouring coffee action, you must be wearing the apron and nothing else—not even shoes or a wig. Then dance.

AUNT ARCTIC SAYS

27

Being a server in the Coffee Shop is a great way to help out, but you won't earn any coins pouring coffee for customers. To get a paying job, waddle over to the bags of java behind the counter to play *Bean Counters*. You'll be paid in coins to catch the bags of coffee beans as they are tossed from the back of the van. Once you've caught the bags, you have to stack them on the platform.

Catch and Carry: You begin each game with three chances to empty all five trucks. Move your mouse left and right to get under each bag and catch it. Drop off the bags on the platform by clicking your mouse. Don't carry more than five bags at a time, or you will collapse under the weight!

Earn Coins: Earn points for every bag you catch and drop at the platform. Every time you empty a truck, the points you earn for catching and dropping off bags will increase. If you empty all five trucks, you will earn bonus coins.

Avoid Falling Objects: If you get hit by an anvil, fish, or flowerpot, you will lose one of your chances to complete the game. If you get hit by an object three times, the game ends, but you get to keep the coins you've earned.

HOW TO
PLAY
MANCALA

HINT

Reading Captain Rockhopper's
journal is the *key* to getting
inside his quarters!

Book Room

It will come as no surprise to learn that the Book Room
has books! But you can also check out the artwork of your
fellow penguins on display. Maybe one day you'll see your
own masterpiece hanging from the Book Room's walls.

In addition to reading books and admiring the art,
penguins can challenge one another in *Mancala* and play
Paint by Letters.

Mancala

Some penguins are shy about playing *Mancala* because it looks sort of complicated. But it really isn't! The best way to learn is to play a few games. You'll be surprised how quickly you get the hang of it.

Find a Friend: Waddle up to a table and join a penguin waiting to get started, or ask a friend to join you.

Capture Stones: The object of this game is to capture stones and put them in your mancala, the big hole on your end of the board. You will take turns with your opponent, trying to capture stones each time. The player who captures the most stones wins.

Develop a Strategy: This takes some practice. Put your mouse over a hole to find out the number of stones in it. Try to plan ahead. If the last stone you drop in a turn lands in your mancala, you will receive a free turn.

If All Else Fails, Click: When it's your turn, click on one of the piles of stones on your side. You'll see how the stones move around the board.

GAME TIP

Try reading the instructions on the wall before you play. That will help, but the best way to get good at *Mancala* is to play a few games.

Here's what I do when I stumble upon a multiplayer game I haven't played before: I watch other penguins play and learn from them. To be a spectator of a game, click on the table while a game is in progress. You'll be confident enough to try it yourself in no time!

AUNT ARCTIC SAYS

PAINT BY LETTERS

If you like to read, this game is for you. You can find it in the Book Room above the Coffee Shop. Go to the bookcase and click on the bookshelf (or click on the red book in the corner of the room). Then click on one of the books with the *Paint by Letters* logo:

Type What You See: When the words appear on a page, start typing them on your computer keyboard. You don't have to worry about capital letters, spaces, or punctuation. If you miss a letter, you won't be able to move on until you type the letter correctly. As you type, an illustration will appear on the opposite page.

Make It Personal: Sometimes, you'll see two or more words together like this: (one/two/three). Type in the word you'd like to use in the story. This will change the pictures you see.

Earn Coins: You have to finish typing the whole book to earn coins. The longer the book, the more coins you will earn. You won't get penalized for typing mistakes.

Bust a Move at the Night Club

As you pass through the doors of the Night Club you are greeted by the sound of thumping bass pounding out of the speakers. Grab a set of headphones and mix beats at the DJ3K machine or move to the music on the dance floor.

If you want to put your dancing skills to the test, you can dance solo or challenge other penguins at the Dance Contest. If the music gets too loud, you can head upstairs to the Dance Lounge. But before you do, run your mouse over the green puffle on the speaker. That little green guy can really groove!

To dance, find the penguin icon on your toolbar and click it. Move your mouse to the picture of a penguin with music notes around it. Click on this box and get ready to shake and shimmy! Or, for a handy shortcut, click outside of your chat bar and press the *D* key on your keyboard.

DANCE CONTEST

SIGN UP!

Where do princesses go to dance?

The *Knight* Club, of course!

Meet Cadence

Occupation: Cadence grooves to her own beat! She's a DJ, musician, artist, dancer, choreographer, and all-around awesome penguin. You'll often find her at the Night Club mixing tracks for penguins to bust a move to. She's one of Club Penguin's best dancers, and break dancing is her specialty.

Fashionista Alert: Cadence is one hip and confident penguin who always sports the coolest looks. She loves to wear bright colors. Her favorite fashion accessory? Her smile!

Nicknames: Fans of Cadence have been known to call her "Dance Machine" and "Mix Master." In fact, she even calls herself that sometimes. She's also known as "DJ K Dance."

What She Can't Live Without: Music!

Philosophy: Cadence is an artist and a true music lover — and she's a DJ, too. She's a free spirit who dances to the beat of her own drum, and she's always got a smile on her face.

Favorite Items: Her green headphones and boom box.

Favorite Types of Music: Funk, techno, classical, trance—Cadence can mix and groove to anything with a solid bass line and a beat.

Parting Words: "I'll see you on the dance floor!"

ROCK 'N' ROLL

PARTY!

DANCE CONTEST

Where do penguins go to dance?

The *snow* ball!

If you're like Cadence and love to boogie, try playing *Dance Contest*—and earn some coins while you're at it! At the Night Club, head over to the table under the poster that says "Dance Contest Sign Up" to begin dancing. You'll need to hit the arrows on your keyboard to make your penguin dance.

Match the Arrows: When the colored arrows rise up to the gray arrows at the top left of your screen, press the matching arrow key on your keyboard. Hold down the key during long arrows for a score bonus.

Combos: Hit a bunch of arrows correctly in a row to get a combo bonus and do some cool dance moves!

Timing is Everything: To score more points, you've got to hit the correct arrow key on your keyboard at just the right moment, when the colored arrows match up with the gray ones.

Just Starting Out?: Choose the "How to Play" option to get a dance lesson from Cadence. Then start on the "Easy" setting, and work your way up to "Hard."

Go Solo or Share the Floor: If you choose "New Game," Cadence will clear the dance floor for you so you can dance by yourself. Or you can groove with other penguins when you select "Multiplayer." If you choose to boogie by yourself, you'll also get to select which song you dance to.

Unlock a hidden level in *Dance Contest!* When you are choosing your difficulty level, click on Cadence. She'll ask you if you'd like to try expert mode. But she'll also warn you that it's very difficult. She's not kidding. It truly is for expert dancers only!

GAME TIP

GAME TIP

If you click on the "Game Upgrades" icon in the Night Club, you'll get the option to buy records you can use while playing *DJ3K*.

Bring your yellow puffle along with you when you play *DJ3K* to earn a coin bonus!

AUNT ARCTIC SAYS

Want to make some music? Waddle over to the DJ table in the Night Club and click on the speakers on the left side of the table to get started. Playing *DJ3K* is a chance to explore the DJ equipment and mix, match, and scratch your way to a musical masterpiece. You get coins for the amount of time you spend making music.

Mix It Up: There is no right or wrong way to play *DJ3K*. All you need to do is play around with the two turntables, the cassette players, and the other equipment to lay down your perfect track.

Hone Your DJ Skills: Click on the different buttons and levers to discover what sounds they create. You'll hear sirens, whistles, car horns, and more! Play around to figure out what combination gets your penguin dancing, and you'll earn extra coins.

FX

Take a Break in the Dance Lounge

If you want to take a break from the excitement of the dance floor, head upstairs to chill out in the Dance Lounge. It's a great place to sit at a table and have a quiet chat with another penguin. It's also where you'll find the arcade games, *Thin Ice* and *Astro-Barrier*. The great thing about them is that you don't have to insert any coins to play— but you can win lots of coins if you've got the skills.

What type of music are balloons afraid of?

Make sure to check out the Dance Lounge whenever a party is happening on the island. It usually gets a fun makeover! In the Music Party of July 2009, the room was transformed into a recording studio, shown here.

Once, there was an *Astro-Barrier* T-shirt on sale in the Penguin Style catalog. The shirt was a very popular item.

THIN ICE

Pop music!

45

THIN ICE

A black puffle that has turned fiery red is the star of this game. Use your keyboard arrows to complete the maze by moving the puffle over blocks of ice. The more ice blocks you melt, the more coins you'll earn.

Move and Melt: At each level there is a different maze, and there are nineteen mazes in all. The object is to move the puffle from the starting point to the end of the maze, which is a red block. As you pass over ice blocks in the maze, you'll melt them. You can't try to pass over these tiles more than once or you'll sink and start the level over again.

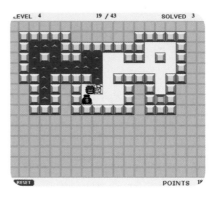

Earn Coins: You can take the easy path each time and finish the maze, but you'll earn more coins if you melt as many tiles as you can.

Special Tiles: Each maze is more difficult than the next. In some mazes, the red tile will be blocked by a locked door and you'll have to find the key before you can exit. As you progress, you'll find light blue, dark blue, and green tiles that all do different things. Move carefully to find out what!

There are coins hidden in the levels of *Thin Ice*. If you complete a level by melting all the ice tiles, a bag of coins will appear in the maze in your next level. Be sure to grab it as you go.

On Level Nineteen there is a false wall in the top right corner of the maze. Move through the false wall until you reach the block with the circle inside it. When you melt this block, an extra bag of coins will appear for every level you have completed. Be sure to grab each bag.

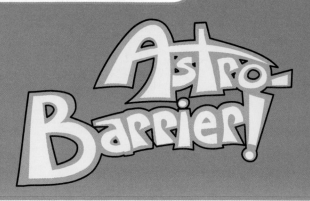

In this game, you'll get to blast away at objects as they fall from space. *Astro-Barrier* can be found in the Dance Lounge next to *Thin Ice*.

Move and Shoot: Press the left and right arrow keys to move your ship. Press the space bar to shoot the moving objects overhead.

Make Every Shot Count: If you run out of bullets on a level, you will lose a turn. If you keep shooting without aiming, your game will be over pretty quickly.

Plan Your Shots: If you hit a target, it becomes a wall, making it harder for you to shoot the other targets. One strategy is to hit the targets on top first, then the ones underneath.

Score Points: You earn ten points for each target you hit, and bonus points each time you clear a level.

You can skip ahead to more challenging levels in *Astro-Barrier*. When you get to the start menu, don't click on "Start." Instead, press the number one on your keyboard to go to Level Ten, or the number two to go to Level Twenty, or the number three to go to Level Thirty.

There are also secret levels in this game. After Level Ten, an instruction box will appear on the screen. Don't hit "Enter" to keep playing. Instead, wait about twenty-five seconds. A blue ship will appear. Shoot it, and you will be taken to the secret levels where you can earn extra points.

Shop Till You Drop at the Gift Shop

If you want a new look or are searching for a way to express yourself, you'll find what you need at the Gift Shop. Open up the Penguin Style catalog to purchase colors, wigs, backgrounds, clothing, and accessories to show other penguins what you're all about.

A new Penguin Style catalog is released the first Friday of every month. Some items are limited edition—they come out once and may return at a later date.

Penguins at Work

Clothing items in Penguin Style aren't only about dressing up. In each catalog a uniform will be featured on the Penguins at Work page. You'll find clothing items for jobs such as a lifeguard, coffee server, firefighter, construction worker, and more. Don't worry—if you don't see clothes for the job you want now, just keep checking.

Change Your Look

The simplest way to give yourself a whole new appearance is to choose a different color for your penguin. You can go from pink to black to aqua in a flash, or just add a fun wig and some cool clothing items.

You can also change the look of your player card by buying different backgrounds. Or buy a country flag for your player card to show where you're from or where you'd love to visit.

Free Items

Club Penguin's shops aren't the only place you'll find items you can use to express your personality.

• There are always free items given away at island-wide Club Penguin parties.

• Captain Rockhopper often gives away free pirate gear when the *Migrator* docks.

• Complete a scavenger hunt to win free prizes.

• Hidden Pins are available every two weeks and can be used to jazz up your player card. (To find out more about Hidden Pins, go to page 227.)

CHECK IT OUT

Need coins to buy that awesome outfit you've got your eye on? Play *Puffle Roundup* to achieve top coin payout!

It's such a thrill when the new Penguin Style catalog is released! I know I'll get to search for the secret items that are hidden inside. They are not always easy to find, but I think searching for them is just as much fun as finding them. Move your mouse over the images on each page and watch for the mouse pointer to change to a hand. When it does, click—you'll be able to see and buy a secret item. The secret items change each month. And you will always find a hidden Viking hat in every catalog.

AUNT ARCTIC SAYS

Anything Goes

Remember, there's no such thing as a "right" or "wrong" outfit. Don't be afraid to combine items from the Penguin Style catalog and the Snow and Sport catalog with free items and costume pieces from the Stage.

The Underground

Beneath the busy streets of Club Penguin are many exciting places to be discovered. Let's leave the surface and check out what's underneath the ice: the Boiler Room, the Underground Pool, and the Mine.

The aboveground Mine Shack and other secret entrances located in the Night Club and the Plaza will lead you to the Underground. Let's begin our tour in the Boiler Room.

Down in the Boiler Room

To get to the Boiler Room, click on the map or use the secret entrance in the Night Club. When you enter the Night Club, click on the fourth speaker on the floor and you will walk down a ladder into the Boiler Room.

Waddle through here to get to the Underground Pool.

Secret passageways are so mysterious, aren't they? You can find one of the secret entrances to the Underground in the Plaza. Click on the manhole cover in front of the Pet Shop to start exploring.

AUNT ARCTIC SAYS

Click here to go to the Night Club.

April Fools' Day

During the 2008 April Fools' Day Party, the Boiler Room became a boiling room—literally! A big vat of boiling water steamed things up in this underground room.

Take a Swim in the Underground Pool

Walk through the green door in the Boiler Room and you'll be in the Underground Pool, also known as the Cave—a cool underwater hangout. You'll see penguins getting their flippers wet in the pool. Feel free to take a dip. You can dive in as you are, but you'll notice that some penguins dress up for a dip in the pool in bathing suits, scuba gear, mermaid costumes, or life jackets and snorkels.

Don't feel like getting wet? Hang out by the side of the pool and watch the strange creatures that swim past the windows. Or climb into the lifeguard chair and watch over your fellow penguins as they splash around.

Why wouldn't the crab share his toys?

Because he was *shell*fish!

CHECK IT OUT

See what happens when you simultaneously press the *E* and *T* keys on your keyboard outside of the chat bar. If you think that's funny, try pressing other letters on the keyboard. There are even more hidden keyboard secrets to discover.

DID YOU KNOW?

In 2007, a crab accidentally broke the glass windows at the pool. The entire Underground flooded! Penguins worked together to drain the flood, and threw a huge water party to celebrate.

After a long day of writing, I love to relax with a refreshing dip in the pool. You, too, can swim in the pool, if you've got the right clothing items. Wear the water wings, inflatable duck, green inflatable duck, or lifeguard uniform, and dance, and you will swim.

AUNT ARCTIC SAYS

Explore the Mine

Don't be afraid to waddle through the dark tunnel on the right side of the pool. It will lead you to the Mine, a shadowy and quiet place. Don't be spooked! You can have a lot of fun here hanging with your pals or playing *Cart Surfer*.

This big, open space is perfect for throwing a party. In fact, this room has gotten some pretty wild makeovers during Club Penguin parties—including the addition of a huge fire-breathing dragon during the Medieval Party! During the Music Jams, penguins could play musical icy stalactites here.

I love scavenger hunts, don't you? That's why I enjoy searching for the new pin hidden somewhere on the island every two weeks. Don't forget to look in the Underground rooms when you're hunting for a pin! I've found some of my favorites in the Underground Pool and the Mine.

AUNT ARCTIC SAYS

CART SURFER

Hop aboard a mine cart for a wild ride! In this fast-paced game you travel at high speeds through the Mine. To play, enter the Mine by walking underground through the Cave or aboveground into the Mine Shack. Then walk into the mining carts.

Away You Go: Not much time to think with this game—as soon as it starts, your cart is off for a wild ride! Hold on tight and try to make it through without tipping over.

Tricky Turns: When you see a turn coming up, lean into it or you'll crash! To lean left, hold down the left arrow key, and to lean right, hold down the right arrow key. Watch out: If you lean for too long, you will wipe out. You get three carts. Once you're out, the game is over.

Mining for Tricks: The secret to scoring big at *Cart Surfer* is to do tricks. Press the space bar to jump and press the up and down arrows to try different moves. But don't try to do a stunt while turning or you will crash! The more tricks you do, the more coins you'll earn.

Cart Surfer is one exciting ride. I've got to hold on to my hat when I play it! I love to try new tricks, but sometimes learning them can be a bit tricky. The best way to figure out how to do different tricks is to try different combinations with your arrow keys and space bar. Here are a few tricks to get you started:

360° Turn: Hit SPACE and then ← or →.
Backflip: Press ↓ and then SPACE.
Handstand: Press ↑ twice.
Rail Run: Hit ↓ twice.
Spin: Press SPACE and then ← or →.

AUNT ARCTIC SAYS

The Mine Shack

If you finish *Cart Surfer*, you will end the game at the Mine Shack. The community garden is located here, too. If you wipe out too many times, you will stay underground! You can only get to the Mine Shack by using the map. You can't waddle to it from another aboveground Club Penguin location.

When the Mine Shack opened in May of year one, mining helmets became available for the first time during a huge Underground party. Penguins discovered that when they danced while wearing their helmets, they could drill into the hard rock. To this day, you can find groups of penguins wearing mining and construction helmets, drilling away wherever something new is being built.

AUNT ARCTIC SAYS

DID YOU KNOW? During one April Fools' party, the shack was turned into a connect-the-dots puzzle. Penguins who finished it found the crayon pin!

The Plaza

THE STAGE

NOW SHOWING

COME AND SEE!

TICKETS

PIZZA

Penguins who love pizza, pets, and plays flock to the Plaza every day.

The first stop is the Pet Shop, where you can adopt a puffle. Next door you'll find the Stage, where you can star in a play or just sit back and watch the show. Then follow the smell of Fish Dish pizza to the Pizza Parlor. You can grab a bite to eat at one of the hottest hangouts on the island.

Adopt a Puffle in the Pet Shop

Puffles make loyal, friendly pets. They come in different colors, and each color puffle has its own personality.

Puffles need to be fed, bathed, taken for walks, and played with. Adopt one, treat it right, and you'll have a friend for life. But if you don't take care of your puffle, it might run away!

Adopting a Puffle: You'll need 800 coins to adopt a puffle. You can adopt as many as sixteen puffles, in every color available. To adopt a puffle, go into the Pet Shop and click on the pen with all the puffles in it. Or click on the red catalog in the lower right corner. Both will open up the Adopt a Puffle catalog. Find the puffle you want, adopt it, and name it. Your new puffle pal will be waiting for you inside your igloo.

Puffle Personalities

Every puffle is different. You can learn a lot about your puffle by playing with it and feeding it.

I really enjoy curling up with a good book, and in the Book Room you can find many wonderful stories to read that are all about puffles! Look in the *Penguin Tales* collection to read some puffle stories written by penguins just like you.

AUNT ARCTIC SAYS

HINT

Certain puffles love to play mini-games! Try taking your pink puffle to *Aqua Grabber*, your red puffle to *Catchin' Waves*, your yellow puffle to *DJ3K*, and your purple puffle to *Dance Contest*.

What kind of pet is the loudest? A trum-*pet*!

Blue Puffle

Attitude: mild-tempered, content, loyal

Favorite toy: ball

Special features: loyal, easy to take care of

Red Puffle

Attitude: adventurous, enthusiastic

Favorite toys: bowling pins, cannon

Special feature: originally from Rockhopper Island

Pink Puffle

Attitude: active, cheery

Favorite toys: jump rope, trampoline

Special feature: loves to exercise

Black Puffle

Attitude: strong, silent type

Favorite toy: skateboard

Special feature: sometimes very energetic

Green Puffle

Attitude: energetic, playful

Favorite toys: unicycle, propeller cap

Special feature: likes to clown around

Purple Puffle

Attitude: a bit of a diva, picky eater

Favorite toys: bubble wand, disco ball

Special feature: loves to dance

Yellow Puffle

Attitude: artistic, spontaneous

Favorite toys: paintbrush, easel

Special features: very creative, dreamer

White Puffle

Attitude: gentle, strong

Favorite toy: skate

Special feature: can turn anything to ice with a breath

Orange Puffle

Attitude: overactive, curious

Favorite toys: box, wagon

Special feature: will eat almost anything

Puffle Personality Test

How can you tell which puffle is right for you? Take the Puffle Personality Test and find out!

Which one of these is your favorite Club Penguin hangout?
   a. the Night Club
   b. the Ice Rink
   c. the Stage
   d. the Coffee Shop
   e. the Dojo
   f. the Beach or the Cove
   g. your igloo
   h. the Snow Forts
   i. the Pizza Parlor

What is your favorite after-school activity?
   a. listening to music
   b. playing any kind of sport
   c. clowning around with friends
   d. drawing or painting
   e. skateboarding
   f. surfing, boating, or swimming
   g. watching television
   h. playing in the snow
   i. eating a snack and then playing with friends

DID YOU KNOW? Each puffle can play in a few different ways. If your puffle's stats are full, it may even play in an extra special way!

76

Out of these jobs, which do you think you'd like the best?
  a. dancer
  b. athlete
  c. comedian
  d. artist
  e. professional skateboarder
  f. pirate
  g. they all sound like fun!
  h. professional ice skater
  i. chef

What do your friends like best about you?
  a. You are a great dancer and are always teaching them the latest moves.
  b. Nothing is dull when you are around—you've got a ton of energy!
  c. You always make them laugh.
  d. You are creative, and you're always thinking of fun things to do.
  e. You don't talk much, but you are a great listener.
  f. You are always taking them on adventures!
  g. Loyal and true, you're everyone's best friend.
  h. You may act quiet and gentle, but you are strong and can help out in a jam.
  i. You're always smiling.

What is your favorite color?
  a. purple
  b. pink
  c. green
  d. yellow
  e. black
  f. red
  g. blue
  h. white
  i. orange

Your Puffle Personality

Mostly As: A purple puffle is perfect for you! These puffles are happiest when they are dancing, so make sure to take your purple puffle to the Night Club.

Mostly Bs: A pink puffle is perfect for you! This active and happy puffle is a great athlete. Take your pink puffle anywhere on the island where there is lots of room to run around!

Mostly Cs: A green puffle is perfect for you! This playful puffle loves to clown around and will keep you laughing.

Mostly Ds: A yellow puffle is perfect for you! This creative puffle likes to paint. You'll love seeing the masterpieces your yellow puffle creates for you.

Mostly Es: A **black** puffle is perfect for you! Quiet and independent, black puffles sometimes like to keep to themselves. But if you like skateboarding as much as black puffles do, they'll be your friend for life.

Mostly Fs: A red puffle is perfect for you! An adventurous penguin like you needs a puffle who is up for anything. A red puffle can explore right along with you and even go surfing with you.

Mostly Gs: A  puffle is perfect for you! Laid-back and loyal, this easy-to-take-care-of puffle is a lot like you. Walk your blue puffle around Club Penguin or just hang out in your igloo. Either way, it will be happy!

Mostly Hs: A puffle is perfect for you! Just like you, this puffle is happiest when the forecast is cold with a chance of snow. Take your puffle to the icy Snow Forts for some quality time together.

Mostly Is: An  puffle is perfect for you! You both are always up for a fun time, especially if it involves snacking on your favorite food. And you're always the life of the party!

If you tied between two letters, don't worry. You'll just have to adopt more than one puffle to make sure you get the perfect pet!

Caring for Your Puffle

Your puffle's player card will let you know if your pet is hungry, healthy, happy, or needs rest. You can give your puffle what it needs by clicking on the symbols on the bottom of the card.

Click on your puffle to view its puffle player card.

These bars tell you if your puffle is hungry, healthy, or tired. The lower the bars, the more attention your puffle needs.

Puffles love to play! It keeps them happy and healthy.

Puffles need rest to keep their energy up.

Puffle Name

ENERGY

HEALTH

REST

You can feed or clean your puffle when you click here.

Healthy puffles love to go for walks—but you can only walk one puffle at a time.

Feed a happy puffle some gum or a cookie and watch it do a special trick!

When your puffle is hungry, a box of Puffle-Os will bring its energy up.

Give your puffle a bath and see what happens!

A Penguin's Best Friend

As long as you take care of your puffle, it will be waiting for you inside your igloo. If you let any of the health bars on your puffle's player card go empty, your puffle will run back to the wild! But don't overdo it. If your puffle's health bars are full, don't feed it or give it a nap, or it will lose health.

Cool Puffle Gear

Puffles are so cute, you're going to want to spoil yours with special items you can find in the catalog in the Pet Shop. Some puffle accessories like beds, water and food dishes, and toys have a secret. When you buy one of these items, it will be put in storage in your igloo. (To learn more about decorating your igloo, go to page 188.)

Add the puffle furniture to your igloo and watch and wait. Your puffle will play with the item all on its own! Remember that you still have to play with your puffle, feed it, and give it a nap to keep it healthy, even if you have these special puffle items.

PUFFLE ROUNDUP

If you love puffles, why not get a job at the Pet Shop? Go to the door marked "Employees" and help herd the puffles back into their pen. You get coins based on how many puffles you can catch in the shortest amount of time.

Start Herding: Use your mouse to guide puffles into the fenced area. If you want the puffle to move right, place your mouse to the left of the puffle. If you want the puffle to go left, put your mouse on the right. Trying to get a puffle to move down? Put your mouse on top of it and move it around! To get a puffle to move up, put your mouse below it.

Be Careful: Puffles can be pretty tricky. Some will run away before you can get them into their pen. Try not to steer the puffle off the screen.

The More You Herd, the More You Earn: A round ends when all the puffles have been herded into their pen or have run away. You can end the game after any round. Keep playing to get lots of puffle herding practice, and earn lots of coins, too!

Enjoy the Show at the Stage

There's a little something for every penguin at the Stage!

Be a leading penguin by taking a role in the latest Stage production. The set will change every time a new play is performed.

Not interested in acting? Sit back and watch the performance in these comfy seats.

Click the buttons and pull the levers to create special effects.

SWITCHBOX 30

It's no secret how penguins get to these stylish seats. Just click on the balcony from the Stage and you'll waddle right up.

Penguins can buy costumes and special backgrounds here.

Open the script and click on the lines to read them onstage.

You don't have to stick to the script. Use the provided script for inspiration—then get creative and come up with your own ideas.

CHECK IT OUT

COSTUMES

SCRIPT

COSTUME TRUNK

How to Put on a Play

Here's what you need to know to put on a spectacular show:

Get Your Buddies Together: Send a postcard inviting your buddies to the Stage. Once you are there, decide which roles everyone will take. To send a postcard, click on the ✉ icon on the top of your screen, then on "new message" to choose a postcard and mail it to a friend.

Be an Actor: It's easy to be an actor at the Stage—you don't have to memorize any lines. Choose which role you want to play, click on the script icon, and click on your lines to read them. To further get into character, use the *Costume Trunk* to outfit yourself for the role.

Be a Director: Every great production needs a director with a vision. If you like taking charge, go to the *Costume Trunk*. Buy a director's cap, put it on, and help guide the actors. You can let them know when to begin and where to stand. (You'll even find lines in the script to give you ideas of what you can say.)

Be a Stagehand: Put the *special* into the special effects of your play by being a stagehand. Waddle over to the Switchbox 3000. Click the buttons and pull the levers to control the set, turn on spotlights, and create special effects.

Be an Usher: Make sure everyone is seated for the big show. You can escort penguins to their seats and show them how to get to the balcony.

Be in the Orchestra: If you own an instrument, you can turn any play into a musical! Find other penguin musicians, then head to the black area in front of the Stage. It's called the Pit.

Be a Ticket Taker: Once you've decided who is doing what, you need an audience to watch your fabulous show. If you'd like to be a ticket taker, hang out behind the ticket window in the front of the theater. When a penguin approaches, ask, "Would you like a ticket?" or just greet them with a smile. You'll soon have curious penguins lining up to check out your play!

Relax and Enjoy the Show: Sit back and be entertained! Let other penguins know if you like the show by using your emotes.

Encore, Encore!

Here's a list of plays that have appeared on the Stage. Which was your favorite?

Once upon a time, this fabulous fantasy transformed the Stage into a fairy-tale forest.

The show must go on, but how can it when a ghost is causing trouble and the leading lady refuses to perform?

When a laser shrinks an absentminded professor to the size of a bug, he gets lost in a giant garden!

Chester gets his flippers on a time machine and steps into it. The rest is *pre*history.

Can an explorer survive breaking bridges, snowball attacks, and crocodiles to discover the mysterious golden puffle statue?

Leaving no fish unturned, Detective Jacque Hammer is on the case to find Ruby's missing valuable gem.

Monkey King searches for the Phoenix Queen's treasure, meeting many interesting characters along the way!

Blast off in search of alien life and adventure on the SS *Astro-Barrier* spaceship.

A giant squid attacks, and it's Shadow Guy and Gamma Gal to the rescue!

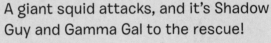

Cheer on your favorite mascot at the mascot tryouts and during an epic dodgeball game.

To fish or not to fish, that is the question. A group of penguins set out to catch a fish that is quite fit for the dish!

Daring Daisy and Fearless Fiesel journey into the mystical depths of the ocean to discover a lost underwater city.

More Things to Do at the Stage

There's no rule that says you have to put on a play at the Stage. Penguins have come up with great ideas for using the Stage in other ways. What ideas can you come up with? Here are just a few:

• Have a snowball fight there.

• Hold a costume contest or a fashion show. Penguin judges use emotes to show if they like or dislike your outfit.

• Use the space for your band practice.

• Hold a poetry reading. Penguins can take turns on the Stage reciting their original poems.

PENGUIN PLAY AWARDS

Penguins were doing such amazing work at the Stage that something needed to be done to recognize them—so the Penguin Play Awards were born! At the first annual Penguin Play Awards, the Stage was transformed into a glamorous theater, complete with a red carpet. Clips from each nominated play were broadcast on screens inside.

A special backstage section hosted a celebrity-studded party. Aunt Arctic and Cadence both made appearances and gave out autographed backgrounds to the lucky fans who happened to meet them. And Aunt Arctic and Cadence both appeared again at the second annual Penguin Play Awards.

Penguins were able to vote, and the big winner for 2009 was *Quest for the Golden Puffle*, which won Best Overall Play, Best Sound, Best Effects, and Best Set. Best Costumes went to *Fairy Fables*. Will your favorite play win next time? Make sure to vote!

KITCHEN

Grab a Bite at the Pizza Parlor

The Pizza Parlor is always hopping with hungry penguins!

Earn coins by making pizza in the kitchen when you play *Pizzatron 3000*.

There's a lot of work to do in the Pizza Parlor. Role-play as the manager or take a job as a waiter, cashier, or a pizza chef.

HINT
Want to toss pizza dough like a pro? Buy a chef's hat when it is on sale in the clothing catalog. Click on the dance action on your toolbar to start tossing pizza dough.

Are you in a band? Grab your instruments and hold a show on the stage here, or play a solo on the piano.

If you're a hungry customer, take a seat. Use the 🍕 when you are ready to eat. A waiter or chef should stop by and take your order.

FISH DISH

Hungry penguins from all over flock to the Pizza Parlor to eat pizzas. You can earn lots of coins if your pizza-making skills are fast enough to feed them!

Order Up: A pizza crust will slide by you on the conveyor belt. It's up to you to add the toppings to get the order right. Look at the order screen in the top right corner to see what kind of pizza you have to make.

The Perfect Pizza: Drag and drop items onto the pizza crust. Your customers will ask for pizza sauce, hot sauce, cheese, seaweed, shrimp, fish, squid, or a combination of these toppings.

Oops: If you made a mistake on a pizza, it won't sell, but you'll get the chance to make it again. If you make five mistakes, penguins will stop buying your pizza and it's game over!

Earn Extra Coins: After you make five perfect pizzas in a row, you start to earn tips from happy customers. Your first tip is ten coins. If you keep making pizzas without making mistakes, you'll get more tips.

Fast Flippers: The pizzas get more complicated the further you get in the game—and the conveyor belt speeds up! Pay attention and move fast to get all your orders done right.

Before you start making pizzas, look for the red lever on the conveyor belt. Click on it and then press start. You'll be making pizzas topped with chocolate sauce, icing, sprinkles, and chocolate chips!

GAME TIP

The Forest

and the Cove

Penguins love to head out into the great outdoors and throw a party! Come with me and I'll show you two perfect party spots: the Forest and the Cove.

You'll find that there's plenty of room for all of your friends in the Forest. The Forest leads to the Cove, the perfect spot for a beach bash extravaganza.

Imagine It All in the Forest

Breathe the fresh, clean air of the forest—a big space with plenty of pine trees to hide behind. It's no wonder that penguins love to play all kinds of games in the Forest. From hide-and-seek to tag to games penguins make up themselves, the Forest is a great place to get creative and have a good time.

Amazing Transformations

The Forest often becomes a different place during monthly parties:

- An octopus sprinkler and waterslide livened up the Forest during the Water Party in year three.

- A huge tree fort with giant plants emerged during the Adventure Party in year four.

- Penguins tapped their feet to the beat at the bluegrass stage here during the Music Party in year four.

- Up, up, and away! Penguins were able to board Gary's hot air balloon from the Forest at the Festival of Flight in year four.

- Penguins stepped right up to the Forest to watch the Great Puffle Circus at the Fall Fair in year four.

Fall Fair

Adventure Party

DID YOU KNOW?

The first yellow puffle was spotted in the Forest during the Halloween Party in year two.

Hang Ten in the Cove

Whether you are looking to work, play, or just relax, look no further. The Cove has it all!

Gather your friends and tell stories around the campfire. You may see some penguins roasting marshmallows on sticks. The sticks were first given away at the Camp Penguin Party held in year two.

If you'd like to help protect the swimmers in the Cove, hop into the lifeguard chair. You can look through the binoculars and watch for any dangers that could be lurking in the sea. Penguins can purchase a lifeguard shirt when it's available in the Penguin Style catalog. You can make your penguin swim if you wear this shirt.

A surf-loving penguin built the Surf Hut once he saw the amazing waves in the Cove, and penguins have been playing *Catchin' Waves* ever since.

HINT

Want to take your puffle surfing? You can if you own a red puffle! Simply take your red puffle for a walk and head to *Catchin' Waves*. It will hang ten on its very own surfboard right next to you!

CATCHIN' WAVES

Cowabunga! Head over to the Surf Hut (the hut that says "Surf" on it) to perform totally tubular tricks. It takes practice to become a good surfer so don't give up.

You can expect to wipe out a few times before you get the hang of it.

Getting Started: Choose from Surf Lesson, Freestyle, Competition, and Survival. If it's your first time, take the Surf Lesson to get warmed up. Practice in Freestyle mode before you move on to Competition and Survival.

Hanging Ten: Use your mouse to steer up and down, lean forward and back, and keep your balance.

Tubular Tricks: Use your keyboard to perform tricks. You can press either the W, A, S, or D keys or the arrow keys while you are surfing. Try pressing different combinations of keys to perform advanced tricks. "Shoot the tube" by surfing very close to the curl of the wave. Don't get too close to the wave or you'll end up wiping out!

Basic Moves:

Wave   W or ↑

Sit   S or ↓

Handstand   A or ←

Dance   D or →

Advanced Moves:

The Lazy Wave   W + S or ↑ + ↓
(Wave + Sit)

Coastal Kick   A + D or ← + →
(Handstand + Dance)

The Backstand   ↓ + A or S + ←
(Sit + Handstand)

Surf Fever   D + W or ← + ↑
(Dance + Wave)

Ice Breaker   A + W or ← + ↑
(Handstand + Wave)

Blender   S + D or ↓ + →
(Sit + Dance)

Earn Coins: The more tricks you do, the more coins you will earn!

Bring Your Own Board

Do you want to surf faster and earn more coins when you play *Catchin' Waves*? Click on the blue note attached to the pink surfboard at the Surf Hut. Buy a Daisy Surfboard or a Flame Surfboard and carry it with you when you play to upgrade your game experience.

The island is filled with many wonderful surprises! Here's one of them. To find the hidden silver surfboard, click on the blue note attached to the pink surfboard at the Surf Hut. Then click on the word *waves* on the top of the note. You'll be given the option to purchase a silver surfboard for 800 coins. Use this board when you play *Catchin' Waves* and you'll soon find yourself flying across the waves at superspeed.

AUNT ARCTIC SAYS

The Forts

and Ice Rink

CLUB PENGUIN
TIME ZONE

Penguins love to be outside, especially when it's cold and snowy out. Let's check out some of the best spots for outdoor activities: the Snow Forts and Ice Rink. Whether you're into sports or just like to play in the snow, you're sure to find some fun in these areas.

Have a Ball at the Snow Forts

In the mood for a snowball fight? Then head to the Snow Forts, pick a fort, and start throwing snowballs. Once a snowball fight begins, other penguins will usually show up to join in the fun.

If you want to practice your aim, you can throw snowballs at the target on the Clock Tower. Gary the Gadget Guy built the snowball-powered clock in 2007. He designed it so when penguins aimed a snowball at the target attached to it, the inner gears would wind up.

The clock is set to PST—Penguin Standard Time. PST might be different than the time on your computer, but every penguin on the island will see the same time on the clock. That makes it easier to meet up with your buddies.

To throw a snowball, click on the ⦿ on your toolbar. A target will appear on the screen. Move the target to the place where you want your snowball, and click. Then watch your snowball fly!

Use a keyboard shortcut to throw snowballs more quickly. Put your cursor over the spot you'd like to hit and press the T key on your keyboard. (Make sure your cursor is not inside the chat bar, or this will not work.) A target will appear. Click to throw a snowball, and then keep pressing T to throw a bunch of snowballs, one after the other.

AUNT ARCTIC SAYS

Get Your Game On in the Ice Rink

Feeling competitive? There's always some kind of game going on at the Ice Rink. Any penguin can play games here. If you'd rather sit on the sidelines, there's always room in the stands for a new spectator. Or buy a cheerleader outfit in the Snow and Sports catalog and cheer on the players!

The games here are just for fun—you can't earn coins by playing them. Most of the time, you'll find the Ice Rink. On occasion, the rink becomes a soccer field to get the Club Penguin soccer season started. And during parties the rink can transform into something completely new. During the Water Party of June 2008, the rink became a giant pool, complete with a waterslide and volleyball net.

CHECK IT OUT

You will see penguins throwing snowballs in other places, even indoors. Around here, it's another friendly way of saying hello. If you're not interested in a snowball fight, simply walk away, or say, "No, thanks."

Ice Hockey and Soccer

Would you rather shoot a puck across an icy surface or dribble a ball on artificial turf? No matter which sport you want to play, these tips will help you start a game:

Suit up: You can purchase uniforms and gear, such as a soccer jersey or hockey stick, in the Snow and Sports catalog. You don't need these to play, but suiting up can help to psych you up!

Find friends: Get the word out to your friends that you want to have a game. You might want to send a postcard to do this.

You don't need two big teams to have fun on the field. You and a friend can have a shoot-out! See who can make the most goals out of ten. A shoot-out is also a great way to determine the winner in a tie game.

GAME TIP

Divide into teams: It helps if each team chooses a color so it's easier to see who's on your side when you pass the ball. If you don't have jerseys, you can change your penguin color.

Get the ball or puck in the goal: Use your mouse to move your penguin toward the ball or puck. Push it into the goal. Choose one penguin from each team to protect your goal. Once a goal is made, the ball or puck will automatically appear in the center.

Keep Score: The team with the most goals at the end of the game wins. You can also just play for fun.

The Beach, the Dock,

and the *Migrator*

The Beach and the Dock are two places you can go if you're craving a little fun in the sun. You can lounge with friends in beach chairs, explore the Lighthouse, fly in *Jet Pack Adventure*, and ride the waves in *Hydro-Hopper*.

Once in a while you'll see Captain Rockhopper's ship, the *Migrator*, docked here. The captain himself comes ashore when he's docked to make new friends. Keep an eye out—you just might spot him.

Hangin' Out at the Dock

Take the path to the right of the Lighthouse. It leads to the Dock, a great place to go fishing, play *Hydro-Hopper*, or just hang out and catch some rays.

The next time Club Penguin has a party, make sure you take time to visit the Dock. It usually features some of the coolest decorations. It's been transformed into a snow castle, a pumpkin patch, and even a stage where musical performances were held.

What did the water say to the boat?

Nothing, it just waved!

HYDRO-HOPPER

Grab a tube and hold on tight as a speedboat tows you in *Hydro-Hopper*! This game used to be known as *Ballistic Biscuit* until September of year two. Waddle over to the speedboat next to the Dock to get started. The object of the game is to avoid obstacles and earn more coins by jumping over anything in your way.

Avoid Sharks: . . . and icebergs, seagulls, floating logs, or anything else in the water. If you don't, you will crash and fall out of your tube. Use your mouse to move and click to jump. Move to the left and right to stay away from drifting objects or jump over them.

Buoy Bother: You can't jump over buoys—they are too tall. Avoid them instead.

Look for Life Preservers: Pick one up to earn an extra life.

Earn Extra Coins: Jumping over an object rather than just steering clear will earn you more coins. Try jumping over two objects in a single jump to earn even more!

You can trade in your tube for a wakeboard. Click on the red note attached to the pink wakeboard (or find it on the bottom right of your screen). Or you can purchase the Pink Striped Wakeboard or Yellow Arrow Wakeboard for three hundred coins. Make sure you are holding it when you go to play *Hydro-Hopper,* and it will change how you play the game.

TO TOP

Click here for a quick way to reach the Beacon at the top of the Lighthouse.

DRUM.

Get Onstage at the Lighthouse

Making music at the Lighthouse is special. Grab an instrument such as a guitar, drums, trombone, or tuba, then dance. The sound of your instrument will join with those of other penguins to play a song.

The Lighthouse stage is also a great place to do a stand-up comedy act. Stand behind the mic and tell your favorite jokes.

Be sure to visit the Lighthouse and Beacon during parties. In December of year three the whole place was transformed into a giant Christmas tree!

CHECK IT OUT

Get a Great View at the Beacon

Walk up the stairs of the Lighthouse to get to the Beacon. Its light guides ships, like the *Migrator*, safely to Club Penguin shores. Look through the telescope to see if Captain Rockhopper's ship—or anything else—is headed toward the island. If you're feeling adventurous, play *Jet Pack Adventure* and zip around the island while zooming high in the sky.

The Beacon is in shipshape now, but back in year one it needed a lot of repairs. Penguins donated their coins to help restore it, and soon it was better than ever. The restoration came just in time: Captain Rockhopper saw the light welcoming him in after a long voyage at sea.

Finding that it's a bit too bright at the Beacon? Click the "off" switch to turn off the light!

Penguins who looked through the telescope during the Festival of Flight in year four saw clouds shaped like ducks, ships, and fish!

JET PACK ADVENTURE

Thanks to Gary the Gadget Guy, penguins are able to take to the skies in the high-flying game *Jet Pack Adventure*. Soar through the skies collecting coins along the way. Whatever coins you get, you get to keep!

Watch Where You Fly: Use your arrow keys to control your jet pack. Try to fly into coins, fuel, and extra jet packs. Avoid obstacles such as coffee bags and anvils. Crashing into them will slow you down and eat up your fuel.

Safe Landing: The only safe areas to land are the designated landing pads at the end of each level.

Look Out Below!: If you run out of jet packs, you will use your parachute to glide safely to the ground. Where you end up depends on what location you were flying over. You could find yourself in the Town, Plaza, Snow Forts, Beach, Iceberg, Mountain, or the Cave. The game ends on the landing pad in the Mine.

Fuel for Thought: Keep your eyes open for extra jet packs—if you catch one you'll get an extra life in case you run out of fuel.

Climb Aboard the *Migrator*!

When Captain Rockhopper the pirate lands on Club Penguin, he docks at the Beach, beside the Lighthouse. Captain Rockhopper prefers traveling only with his trusty first mate, Yarr, but he allows penguins to visit his ship when he's docked. If you've ever been on the ship, you know that different parts of the *Migrator* have different names. Here's a list of sailor lingo to help you find your way around!

Deck: The top floor of the ship. Stand behind Captain Rockhopper's steering wheel and imagine you are sailing to an exciting new destination.

Mast: The tall pole that holds up the ship's sails.

Jolly Roger: The flag on a pirate ship. You'll know the *Migrator* has been through stormy weather if the flag is tattered.

Crow's Nest: The small platform on top of the mast. You will often see Yarr, Captain Rockhopper's puffle, bouncing up and down near the Crow's Nest.

Hold: The area belowdecks. Check out the hold to see if Captain Rockhopper is selling or giving away any treasures he's found on his journey.

Captain's Quarters: The room where the captain works and sleeps. Look for the key to this room in Captain Rockhopper's journal, which can be found in the Book Room. Once you're inside, you can play *Treasure Hunt*.

Treasure Hunt

Captain Rockhopper finds so many amazing treasures on his travels that he created this game so he can share them with other penguins. The key to success is cooperation.

Find the Key: Want to get into Captain Rockhopper's quarters so you can start searching for treasure? Head to the Book Room and read Captain Rockhopper's journal. You'll find the key there.

Dig It: The game takes place in a box of sand. You and your friend take turns digging up squares of sand in the box. If you dig in the right spot, you will uncover treasure!

Coins and Jewels: Be on the lookout for these treasures while digging. Red rubies are worth twenty-five coins, a gold coin is worth one, and the rare green emerald is worth one hundred. To earn your reward, you have to uncover each coin or jewel completely.

Work Together: If your friend digs up a piece of a jewel, make sure to dig next to that piece on your turn. It's the only way to completely uncover the treasure.

GAME TIP

Look for a sparkle underneath the sand. It's a clue that there may be a jewel or coin buried there.

Just like any other penguin, I become excited when I hear that Captain Rockhopper is coming to the island. I enjoy looking at the Notice Board in his quarters to see photos from his thrilling adventures and to find out what he has planned next. I especially look forward to the arrival of autumn, when the captain brings exciting new surprises for the Fair. Things always get more interesting on Club Penguin when Captain Rockhopper visits us!

AUNT ARCTIC SAYS

DID YOU KNOW?

In December of year five, when players dug for treasure they found candy canes and peppermint candies!

Meet Rockhopper

Occupation: Pirate captain of the *Migrator*, the finest ship to ever sail the seven seas

Where He Calls Home: This sailor may hail from Club Penguin, but his heart belongs to the sea.

Best Matey: His puffle, Yarr, a true-blue friend with bright red fur

Most Memorable Discoveries:
- Findin' a mess o' red puffles
- Landin' on the fine shores of Rockhopper Island

Favorite Sayings:
- "Captain Rockhopper is me name, and treasure is me game."
- "Chin up, sailor! There be fair winds on the horizon."
- "Avast and away! It be time to weigh anchor, but I promise to return."

When He's Not Sailing, You Can Find Him:
- Darin' daily dangers
- Discoverin' treasure
- Drinkin' drums o' cream soda

Bet You Didn't Know:
Captain Rockhopper built the *Migrator* with his own bare flippers.

Meet Yarr

Occupation: As first mate of the *Migrator*, Yarr helps make sure the ship smoothly sails the seas.

Special Talent: This brave buccaneer has a gift for surfing the ocean waves.

Where You'll Find Him: When he's not hanging in the Crow's Nest and shooting snowballs out of the cannon, he's exploring Club Penguin with his captain.

Bet You Didn't Know: Yarr got his name because he answered every time Captain Rockhopper cried out, "Yarr!"

DID YOU KNOW?

Captain Rockhopper discovered red puffles on an adventure in year one. The puffles liked Captain Rockhopper so much that they hopped onboard the Migrator and sailed with him to Club Penguin. Now you can adopt one at the Pet Shop!

HINT

When Captain Rockhopper is visiting Club Penguin, the best places to look for him and Yarr are the Migrator, Dock, Iceberg, Beach, and Pizza Parlor. If you find him and ask him to be your buddy, he will give you a signed photo of himself.

PIRATE TREASURE

Captain Rockhopper's Treasures

When Captain Rockhopper finds treasure, he doesn't keep it all for himself. He brings a lot of it to Club Penguin with him and sells it from the ship. Sometimes, he even gives away free items. All of these items are special, but here's a closer look at some favorites that make us say yo-ho-ho!

Red Pirate's Bandana: Wear this classic item, and everyone will instantly know you're a pirate at heart.

Sailor Shirt: If you want to join a pirate crew, this shirt's a must.

Captain's Coat: You can strut around like Captain Rockhopper in this coat that demands attention.

 Pirate Dress: Fine fashion for any pirate lass.

 Treasure Chest: Every pirate needs his own treasure! But you don't have to bury yours— you can proudly display it in your igloo.

 Pirate Ship: If you can't sail with Captain Rockhopper on the *Migrator*, owning this magnificent model is the next best thing.

 Ancient Penguin Monument: This unusual item brings the islands right into your igloo.

 Stuffed Parrot: Just like the real thing, and you don't have to feed it crackers!

 Sea Monster Player Card Background: Liven up your playing card with this friendly creature from the deep.

 Plantus Fantasticus, Surprisus Maximus, and Sprouting Spectaculous: These potted plants surprised everyone on Club Penguin when they slowly began to grow . . . and grow . . . and grow . . .

The Ski Village

EVERYDAY
PHONING
FACILITY

The Ski Village is a great place to find both indoor and outdoor activities. Whether you're a sports fanatic or a couch potato, there's something in the Ski Village for you.

Feel like racing down a snowy slope? Then check out the Ski Hill. In the mood to earn some coins? Try some *Ice Fishing*. If you'd rather stay inside, you can always chill in the Ski Lodge.

Gear Up

Before you head to the Ski Hill for some outdoor action, you might want to suit up. Click on the Snow and Sport catalog located at the Ice Rink. There are items here you won't find in the Penguin Style catalog.

Everyone on Club Penguin can purchase a sports-themed player card background. You can buy everything from sports clothing or equipment to even sports furniture for your igloo.

New items appear in each catalog, but don't worry if you don't see an item you need. Older items are brought back all the time, so keep checking. And make sure you move your cursor over every item or word on each page — you might just uncover a hidden item.

Why did the coach go to the bank?

To get his quarterback!

Sports Gear

Here are just some of the things sports fans can expect to find in the catalog:

Football fans: Footballs, helmets, and jerseys

Hockey fans: Sticks, helmets, and jerseys

All sports jerseys, uniforms, and cheerleader outfits come in red, blue, and green, so you and your friends can choose a team color. And there's good news— yellow uniforms are coming soon!

AUNT ARCTIC SAYS

Soccer fans: Jerseys

Baseball fans: Baseball gloves, uniforms, matching baseball caps

Fishing fans: Hats, fishing rods

Referees: Whistles, striped referee shirts

Cheerleaders: Cheerleading uniforms, side-tied style wigs

Job seekers: Lifeguard shirts, rescue squad uniforms

Other equipment: Tennis rackets, treadmills, gym mats, exercise balls, exercise bikes

Join the Rescue Squad!

You may find a Rescue Squad uniform in the pages of the catalog. Penguins who wear this uniform are doing more than making a fashion statement—they're helping to keep Club Penguin safe.

Rescue Squad teams began by patrolling Ski Hill, and then the squads appeared all over the island, ready to spring into action if a disaster strikes. If a Rescue Squad penguin warns you that an earthquake or storm is coming, follow them to a safe place.

CHECK IT OUT

Form a squad with your friends. Arrange to meet at a specific time and location and patrol the area, looking for penguins who need help.

If you are wearing the Rescue Squad uniform and helmet and nothing else, use the wave action. Your penguin will hold up the Rescue Squad sign, notifying those around you that you are there to help.

The strong yet stylish helmet protects the Rescue Squad member in dangerous situations.

Insulated material keeps Rescue Squad members warm in the most frozen conditions.

The Ski Hill is pretty impressive, but it isn't the tallest mountain on Club Penguin. That honor goes to . . . the Tallest Mountain! All penguins got to visit this high point during the Festival of Flight in year four by getting a ride in Gary's hot air balloon.

RIDGE RUN

Hold on to your snow hat! This run is super steep and loaded with obstacles.

PENGUIN RUN

Can you say wipeout? This tricky run is loaded with traps to trip you up.

Get Ready to Race at the Ski Hill

If you're anxious for some winter sports action, hop on the Ski Lift to be carried to the top of the Ski Hill. This spot has one of the best views on Club Penguin. But the main reason penguins come here is to have sled races against one another. You can't race alone, so if the Ski Hill is empty, send a "Sled Race" postcard to a buddy who's online at the same time as you. Ask them to join you for a race.

A red snow tube is standard for a sled race, but penguins can slide down the snowy hill on a toboggan or sled if they choose. Click on the green note tacked to the toboggan to buy a toboggan or green or pink sled for three hundred coins each. You can also use a GT sled. Just click on the sled at the top of the Ski Hill. Make sure you are holding your special sled when you enter the race.

AUNT ARCTIC SAYS

Need to practice? Do the bunny hop right over to this easy hill!

BUNNY HILL

EXPRESS

The perfect run for penguins with a need for speed.

Sled Racing

Whether you're in the mood for an easy glide or feel like sliding at superspeed, there's a sled race for you!

Find a Race: Walk to one of the sled runs. The Bunny Hill is the easiest run and best way to learn the game. Ridge Run is the most difficult. The race can't begin until enough penguins join in, but if you wait a little bit you'll usually find a racing partner.

Don't Wipe Out: Use your arrow keys to move left and right as you speed down the hill. Avoid obstacles such as a log or tree branch. If you hit one, you will wipe out. But you'll quickly get back on your snow tube and continue racing.

Finish First: The race ends when all penguins cross the finish line. You will earn coins depending on how you place in the race.

Sled Racing is a wonderful way to make new friends. Don't be shy—approach a penguin on the Ski Hill and ask them to join you in a race.

AUNT ARCTIC SAYS

Want to zoom past your opponents? Slide over an ice patch to go extra fast!

GAME TIP

149

This legendary big fish can be caught while playing *Ice Fishing*.

MULLET

Every half hour the cuckoo clock chimes and a yellow bird pops out and yells, "Cuckoo!" The bird's name is Fred.

Warm Up in the Ski Lodge

After a day of playing winter sports, there's nothing like relaxing in front of a warm fire. You'll find one inside the Ski Lodge. This rustic log cabin is filled with comfy couches and some interesting wall hangings, including a moose head and a cuckoo clock. Pass the time here by playing *Find Four* or *Ice Fishing*.

ICE FISHING

This slow-paced game is a nice way to relax and earn coins at the same time. To play, head to the door marked "Gone Fishing" at the back of the Ski Lodge.

Catch Fish!: You must have a worm on the end of your hook to catch a fish. Move your mouse up and down to raise and lower your hook. When you see a fish, lower your hook to the fish and catch it. Raise your hook above the ice and click your mouse to release the fish.

Avoid Obstacles: Barrels and boots can kick fish off your line. Jellyfish, sharks, and crabs will cost you a worm if they touch your line.

Watch Your Worms: If you lose a worm, raise your hook above water level and click on the can of worms to get a new one. Once you lose all three of your worms, the game is over. Before that happens, try to catch a can of worms to get an extra life.

Collect Your Coins: At the end of the game, you will receive one coin for every fish you catch. If you catch the extra-big Mullet at the end, you will get an extra fifty coins.

GAME TIP

Click on the blue note by the fishing poles to buy a Flashing Lure Fish Rod for two hundred coins. Hold it with you when you play, and you'll be able to catch gray fish worth eight coins each! The gray fish are tricky to catch—some are super fast, and others will dive to the bottom to avoid your hook.

Many penguins are puzzled about how to capture the Mullet at the end of the game. First, you must catch sixty fish. Then, catch one of the lone fish that swims by, and leave it on the end of your hook. Leave it in the water when the Mullet appears, and see what happens!

AUNT ARCTIC SAYS

Hide Out in the Lodge Attic

Looking for a spot to chat with a friend? The Lodge Attic is perfect. There are more *Find Four* games up here, so why not have a tournament to determine the ultimate champ?

Like many attics, this space sometimes holds some unusual surprises. After the big snowstorm in year two, the extra snow was stored in the Lodge Attic and then used for the Festival of Snow. During the Medieval Party in year four, the room became the top floor of a pink castle. Sunlight streamed through stained glass windows, blue water bubbled from indoor fountains, and the old rocking horse was transformed into a white beauty. Who knows what will find its way into the Lodge Attic next?

Find Four

Looking for something to do with your buddy? Why not play a game of *Find Four*? Once you learn the rules, it's easy to master.

Find a Partner: Walk to a game table to challenge a partner who's sitting there, or wait for someone to challenge you.

Get Four in a Row: The object of the game is to be the first player to stack four round game pieces of the same color in a row: either up and down, across, or diagonally. When the game starts, your name will be highlighted when it is your turn to play. Click on the slot that you would like to drop your piece in. You and your opponent will take turns until one of you gets four pieces in a row.

Find Four is a game of strategy, not speed! Before you make a move, think about how you can win *and* block another player from winning at the same time.

The Iceberg

This huge chunk of ice floats in the waters outside Club Penguin. You can't walk there—instead, click on the map on your screen. You'll see the Iceberg in the upper right-hand corner of the screen, just past the Cove. It's not marked. Click on it to go there.

With no furniture or buildings to get in the way, a whole lot of penguins can gather here and move around easily. That may be why the Iceberg is the most popular party spot on Club Penguin. It's also the site of the Aqua Grabber. This underwater machine was invented by Gary the Gadget Guy.

Click on this magnificent mini submarine to play *Aqua Grabber*.

Penguins ask me all the time if the Iceberg rumor is true. I must be honest and say that I have never known it to tip over. However, anything is possible!

Party at the Iceberg

You're hanging out in town when penguins start spreading the word: "Party at the Iceberg!" Curious, you head to the Iceberg and find a crowd of penguins there, dancing and talking. Some are even wearing helmets and using jackhammers to break into the ice!

What's it all about? Well, rumors have been swirling around Club Penguin for a long time that it's possible to tip the Iceberg. So penguins hold Iceberg parties, trying to get it to tip. There are many ways to take part in one of these parties.

Dance: Some penguins think that if enough penguins dance, the motion will tip the Iceberg.

Drill: To use a jackhammer, you need the construction or miner's helmet. Sometimes they are given away when a big construction project is happening on the island. If you have a membership, you can sometimes purchase them in the Penguin Style catalog. Wear the helmet and nothing else. Then dance and drill away!

Follow the Crowd: Join lots of penguins on one side of the Iceberg to see if it will tip.

Chant: Start a rousing chant of "Drill! Drill! Drill!" or "Tip the Iceberg!" to get other penguins moving. Another popular chant is "Dance or drill, just don't stand still!"

I love to play games with my puffles, don't you? If you have a pink puffle, take it for a walk and then play *Aqua Grabber*. Your puffle will appear in the game with you wearing scuba gear, and will swim alongside you as you search for treasure.

AUNT ARCTIC SAYS

Explore the ocean depths by climbing in and taking the controls of the Aqua Grabber. You can pilot this machine as you hunt for treasure on the sea floor.

Move Around: Use ⬆️, ⬇️, ⬅️, and ➡️ to move up, down, left, and right. Press SPACE to operate the grabber's claw and to drop or pick things up. Be careful not to bump into things, or you'll run out of air more quickly. You'll be searching for pearls, treasure chests, and soda barrels.

Grab the Goods: Each blue oyster contains a pearl. Wait until the oyster falls asleep before catching the pearl.

Net Your Treasure: Small items can fit right on the Aqua Grabber, but if you grab big items, like the treasure chest, you need to bring it to the net. Be careful—if you bump into something, you'll drop what you're carrying.

Get Some Air: Look for large air bubbles you can move over to fill up with extra oxygen. Large bubbles flow out of a vent on the ocean floor. You can also get air by going above the surface of the water.

To clear the first level, you'll need to defeat a special clam and steal its giant pearl. Try to trick the clam by switching the pearl with a rock that's the same size and shape.

GAME TIP

163

The Dojo

Penguins thought this was just a mountain—but a volcano inside the mountain awakened, and ninjas began the path to train to master the element of fire.

Two peaceful puffle statues flank the stone steps of the Dojo. Sensei built this beautiful building so aspiring ninjas could have a place to train. Inside, Sensei trains penguins in the art of *Card-Jitsu*.

The Dojo is surrounded by the three elements: water, fire, and snow. Water flows from the waterfall, fire burns deep inside the volcano, and frozen snow covers the mountainsides.

Train Inside the Dojo

The Dojo training room is where penguins learn the ancient art of *Card-Jitsu*. They face one another to train and win belts on the way to earning the ultimate prize: a black belt, and the honor of becoming a full-fledged ninja.

LEGEND

INSTRUCTIONS

Earn a white belt first and then work your way up to a black belt.

You can practice *Card-Jitsu* with a partner on one of these mats. However, you'll earn belts faster if you ask Sensei to match you with an opponent.

Sensei built the Dojo by himself a long time ago. Then he spent a long time in the wilderness, seeking wisdom. In November of year four he returned to the Dojo to teach others the way of the ninja.

Want to talk to Sensei? Pass your cursor over the cushion and he will appear. Sensei will set you up in matches with other penguins so you can earn your belts. You can battle Sensei at any time, but you won't have a chance at beating him until you've earned your black belt.

Card-Jitsu

The mist flowing from the pot changes to reflect the three elements of *Card-Jitsu*: water, snow, and fire.

Click on the cards to see how far you've progressed in your quest to become a ninja.

Meet Sensei

Sensei is a man who speaks simply, yet his words say great things. He often speaks in haiku, an ancient form of Japanese poetry. Each poem is three lines long. The first and last lines have five syllables each, and the second line has seven syllables. In honor of Sensei, this profile is written in haiku.

Occupation:
He built the Dojo
to train young penguin ninjas.
He is one who guides.

Favorite Food:
In praise of sushi!
Raw fish is so delicious.
It tastes of the sea.

Favorite Beverage:
Drink your tea slowly.
Enjoy every sip you take.
It will calm the mind.

Where You Can Find Him:
High in the mountains
is where he built the Dojo.
Here he is at peace.

What He Does for Fun:
Oh fortune cookie,
What words do you have for me?
I wrote them myself.

Why He May Surprise You:
Sensei may look mild,
but face him in a battle.
He's one great ninja!

Card-Jitsu ™
Trading Card Game

To master this game, you must understand the elements: water, snow, and fire.

Know the Elements: Think of *Card-Jitsu* as a game of rock-paper-scissors, but with cards. Water douses fire, fire melts snow, and snow freezes water. You and your opponent each throw a card. The dominant element wins the hand. So, if you throw a fire card and your opponent throws snow, you win the hand. The winning card will appear on the screen above your player.

Numbers Count: Let's say you both throw the same element. In that case, the card with the highest number wins. So if you throw three ice but your opponent throws five ice, your opponent wins the hand.

Collect Colors: To win *Card-Jitsu*, you need to win at least three rounds. But there's a twist. You must have one card of each element, but each card must be a different color. Or, you can have three cards of the same element as long as they are all different colors.

Use Logic: Don't know what to throw? Try throwing out cards with the highest number value first. As you learn the game, you can use logic to anticipate your opponents' moves. Let's say your opponent has earned one yellow fire card and one green water card. They need an ice card to win. Since you know that fire melts ice, you can throw a fire card to stop them from winning.

Know Your Special Cards: When certain cards are played, they'll change the rules for the next hand. The border of these cards will glow when they appear on your screen. Run your cursor over the card to read the new rule. That way you'll be able to determine the best move to make on your next turn. If your opponent plays a special card and wins the hand, look for a symbol on top of your screen that will show you the rule change.

You can buy *Card-Jitsu* cards in stores or in the Club Penguin shop online, outside the game. You'll get unique power cards with special animation when you use them in the game. The best part is that your new cards will help you earn belts faster!

GAME TIP

Throw a snowball at a gong and see what happens!

Journey to the Ninja Hideout

A black ninja mask
gains entrance to the hideout.
There is more to learn . . .

Once you have earned your black belt, walk to the stone wall to the left of the main Dojo entrance. The door will open to reveal the secret entrance to the Ninja Hideout.

Here, you can learn more about Sensei, buy ninja gear, and play *Card-Jitsu* with other black belts. It is also where you begin the next phase of your journey. From the Hideout, a ninja can access three different paths and learn how to master the elements.

Step into Flying Flippers Emporium and purchase special gear from the Martial Artworks catalog. This is where you'll find the Amulet that unlocks the doors to the elemental paths.

You need an Amulet to continue your journey by following the paths of water, snow, and fire here.

Penguins can buy a complete ninja outfit in the catalog. Combine the ninja outfit, your ninja mask, and the Cloud Wave Bracers to perform this amazing ninja skill: If you're wearing all three things and wave, your penguin will vanish into a shadowy form. The effect stops once you begin walking.

DID YOU KNOW?

Mastering the Elements

Amulets in hand,
water, fire, and snow are yours.
The journey begins . . . .

Fire Dojo

A pit of molten lava bubbles underneath the ninjas who train on the fire path. Those ninjas who can take the heat learn how to master fire's boundless energy by playing *Card-Jitsu Fire*. If you have questions about this fiery path, Sensei can give you advice.

Your Reward

As you battle on the fire path, you will earn four pieces of a Fire Suit. You must master the element before you can complete your suit. Once you have all four pieces of your suit, you can challenge Sensei to earn a special gem.

Go to the mats if you want to play another player in Practice Mode. But you'll earn pieces of your Fire Suit faster if you ask Sensei to set up a battle for you.

CHECK IT OUT

Card-Jitsu Fire

In this game of skill and luck you can test your fire abilities against as many as three other ninjas.

Be Prepared: To play, you'll need a ninja mask, which you earn by playing *Card-Jitsu*. Then you need an Amulet, which you can buy in the Martial Artworks catalog. When you're equipped, talk to Sensei inside the Ninja Hideout. He'll give you a fire booster deck to play with.

Get Fired Up: Click on the fire tablet to open the door to the Fire Room. Once you're inside, talk to Sensei and tell him you want to earn your Fire Suit. You may face up to three opponents.

Pick a Square: Click on one of the stones that appears in the lava pit. Two of the squares surrounding the pit will light up. Click on the square to determine what kind of battle you will have—fire, water, snow, classic *Card-Jitsu*— or choose your element.

You might be tempted to use playing cards with high points as soon as they appear. But those cards may come in handy when you're low on energy. Think about saving them until you really need them. But more importantly—find a strategy that works for you and stick with it!

GAME TIP

Choose a Card: You must play the element on the square you've chosen—highest card wins the battle. When it's your opponent's turn, that ninja will get to choose the element.

Classic *Card-Jitsu*: If you choose the *Card-Jitsu* square you will battle another player in this classic game.

Watch Your Energy: If you lose a battle, you will lose one energy point. The player to hold on to their energy points the longest earns first place.

The EPF is Born

SCANNER

ELITE PEN

Old Headquarters

Secret agents used to work out of the Penguin Secret Agents Headquarters. Then a power-hungry polar bear named Herbert trashed the place with a giant popcorn machine. Another classified agency, the Elite Penguin Force, took over secret agent operations. Now all agents work for the EPF.

Fearless in the face of danger, the EPF keeps a watchful eye over the citizens of Club Penguin, facing peril and danger at every turn.

Mission Impossible?

Even the smartest secret agents can get stuck trying to figure out how to complete the missions successfully. These tips can help you breeze through your missions with a bit more ease.

- In some missions, you can click on the map on the upper left of your screen to get around Club Penguin. Places marked with an *X* are places important to your mission.

- Keep your eyes out for messages written in the secret agent code. You will always find the code bar on the bottom of your screen for easy decoding.

- Remember that you have tools in your spy phone. If something needs to be moved or fixed, try using one of the tools on it.

- When you go to a new place, click around to see if you can pick up any objects. Put every object you find into your inventory—you may need it later! (Keep in mind that there is a limit to how many objects will fit in your inventory.)

- Talk to everyone you see. If someone asks you for help, it's a good idea to help them. You may get an extra reward in the end.

- Objects in your inventory can be combined to make new objects. If none of the tools you have can get a job done, try combining two of them and see what happens.

- If at first you don't succeed, try, try again! If you're stuck in one place, go back to the last place you visited and look around to see if you missed anything. If you were asked to make a choice the first time, try making a different choice this time and see what happens.

Meet Gary

Occupation: Among other things, Gary the Gadget Guy, also known as G, is Club Penguin's resident inventor. Like many other penguins, Gary also has a secret identity. Gary creates all of the equipment EPF field agents use to keep Club Penguin safe. He also acts as mission coordinator.

What You Might Be Surprised to Learn: Gary has an extensive collection of pins that he keeps in his office. If you ever have the chance to go there, look around and see if you can find them.

Is It Possible to Meet Gary?: Gary is always busy creating new things, and he doesn't enjoy big crowds. He's more interested in tinkering with tools than going to the latest parties. But penguins got a chance to meet him at the Festival of Flight, when he was fixing the windows in the Underground Pool, and at the Penguin Play Awards. He's also been spotted at the Halloween parties.

Favorite Food: Pizza. (It's why he invented the Pizzatron 3000.)

Favorite Beverage: When secret agents meet with G, they'll often find him with a cup of coffee in his flipper. It helps him stay up late to work on his inventions.

Gary's Greatest Inventions

Here's a list of some of Gary's most important inventions. When Gary comes out with something new, you can usually read about it in *The Club Penguin Times*. And if he invents something as G for the EPF, agents will get a chance to try it—and sometimes even test the items out for him.

Spy phone

Jet pack

AC 3000 cooling system

Pizzatron 3000

Snowball-powered clock

Life preserver shooter

Crab Translator 3000

CRAB TRANSLATOR 3000

PLEASE SPEAK CLEARLY INTO THE MIC.

THIS MESSAGE

Furensic Analyzer 3000

Aqua Grabber

Flare Flinger 3000

Island Lifter 3000

Monster Maker 3000

Spotted in Gary's Gadget Room: Thingamajig 3000, night-vision goggles, robotic penguin (known as Wheel Bot to penguins in the EPF), prototype sled, super helium

TEST CHAMBER

Hiding Places

Ready for a game of hide-and-seek? There are a few places on Club Penguin where you can hide and see other penguins but they won't know you are there.

Waddle over to the Pizza Parlor and walk toward the pizza oven. Some sacks of flour are stacked up in the corner on the floor. Stand behind them and nobody will be able to see you. You can also become invisible in the Mine if you go behind the icy stalagmite on the lower left of the screen. Next time you are at the Cove, try hiding behind the rocks near the Surf Shack.

Now that you know the best hiding spots on the island, challenge your friends to a game of hide-and-seek. Maybe you'll discover even more great hiding places!

Igloo

Igloo, sweet igloo! Let's take a look at the places that every penguin on the island calls home. In this section you'll find out all the possible ways you can decorate your igloo—and get great tips on how to turn your igloo into a place that really shows your personality.

Let's Get Started

Ready, set, shop! You can decorate your igloo any way you want. First, you'll need coins to purchase items from the catalogs. You won't find these catalogs in any store. They're right inside your igloo so you can shop from the comfort of your own home.

First go to your igloo by clicking on the 🐚 icon in the toolbar on the bottom of your screen.

Once you are inside your igloo, click on the 📏 icon to start decorating. A bunch of new icons will appear.

In addition to buying new flooring for your igloo, you can completely change its design by clicking on the 🔒 icon. Tree house, theater, restaurant, castle, and gym are just some of the styles you can choose from.

Click on the 📕 icon to find everything you need to decorate your space: furniture, electronics equipment, pictures and posters for the walls, rugs for the floors, and more!

When you buy an item, it goes inside the storage box. Click on the 📦 icon to open it.

If you own a jukebox or stereo, you can play music in your igloo. Click on the 📼 icon to select the perfect mood music for your space.

When you are finished making changes to your igloo, make sure you click on the 💾 icon. It will save all your changes.

Do you like the idea of opening up your igloo to any penguin who wants to drop by and say hi? Click on the 🔒 icon when you are in your igloo. Doing this will add your igloo to the map so other penguins in your server can visit.

When you upgrade your igloo to a different design, all your furniture and stuff gets put back in storage. Don't panic when you see your new igloo and it looks empty! Click to open the storage box. You'll find everything there.

I must confess that I am passionate about decorating my igloo—and it's a little cluttered because of all the great things I find in the Better Igloos catalog! I also love to search for hard-to-find items. Each catalog always has a secret item or two hidden inside. To find it, move your mouse around all the objects you see until a little hand appears. Then click.

AUNT ARCTIC SAYS

Decorate Your Igloo

Whether you've bought new items or have some free items you can use, you're ready to decorate your igloo. Here's how to do it:

- Click the 🧵 icon, then the 📦 icon. You'll find all your items that you haven't placed yet in your igloo here. The items in the box are arranged by category: furniture, stuff that hangs on walls, floor coverings, and puffle furniture.

- Select the item you want to add to your igloo and then click on it. It will be added to your room. Click on the item again and move your mouse to place it where you would like it, then click to drop it.

- You can rotate your item to face a different direction. Press ⬅ and ➡ to do so.

- Some items have cool features. Click on an item and then press the up and down arrow keys on your keyboard to see if anything happens. Doing this will change the channels on a television set or light a fire in your fireplace. Experiment to see what else your stuff can do.

- Happy with where your furniture is placed? Stop clicking and leave it where it is. If you are finished, click the 🖫 icon to save your changes.

- If you would like to remove an item from your igloo, simply drag it outside of your igloo when you are in edit mode. It will stay in storage until you need it again.

Awesome Igloo Items

These popular items can be found in igloos all over Club Penguin. If you don't see them in the current catalog, don't worry. There's a good chance they'll pop up in a future catalog.

 Bowling Alley: Bowl over your buddies with these cool items!

 Garden: Got a green thumb? Grow pumpkins, carrots, flowers, and more.

 **Dance Floor:** Nothing gets penguins in the mood to dance more than a brightly lit floor like this one.

 Puffle Posters: Can't get enough puffles? Hang these posters on your wall to show everyone your love for these cute little pets.

CHECK IT OUT

A few times a year, Club Penguin holds igloo-decorating contests. You can find out about them by reading *The Club Penguin Times*.

 Jukebox: Liven up your igloo with some tunes.

Tea Table: Get out of the cold and relax with a hot cup of tea. Only ninjas can buy this item.

Treadmill: Perfect for penguins who like to keep moving.

Popcorn Machine: Nothing beats the smell of freshly popped popcorn wafting through your igloo.

Royal Throne: Sit down in style with this chair that's fit for a king or queen.

Why didn't the penguin wear snow boots?

Because they would melt!

Extreme Igloos

In your travels around Club Penguin, you may see some igloos that make you go, "Wow! How'd they do that?" The answer is, of course, lots of coins—but even more than that, creativity. Check out other penguins' extreme igloo styles. Maybe they'll inspire you to create an extreme igloo of your own!

Table for Two?

Add some tables and chairs, some screens for privacy, and a comfy couch in the waiting area, and you can create your very own restaurant!

Santa's Workshop

Everyone loves to decorate their igloo for the holidays, but some creative penguins take their Christmas decorations to a whole new level. Piles of toys and presents give an igloo the feel of a toy workshop. Red velvet ropes leading to a big chair give penguins a place to wait and say hello to a penguin dressed as Santa.

"Paintball" Paradise

Arrange tall pet towers and cabinets to make the twists and turns of a classic paintball arena. Of course, you and your friends will be playing with snowballs instead!

Open Wide!

Visiting the dentist usually isn't fun—unless you're going to an igloo decorated to look like a dentist's office! A desk, computer, and comfy chairs make up the waiting room. The dentist goes to work in a room with sinks and cabinets. A white picket fence divides up the different rooms.

Pufflemaniacs

Some puffle owners devote their entire igloo space to their special pets. Many of them cover the walls with puffle posters. Then they raid the Love Your Pet catalog for cool puffle toys. They load up their igloo with all the beds, scratching posts, toys, and dishes that they can fit. The puffles love to play with these toys, but there is barely room for a penguin to waddle in these puffle palaces!

Media Madness

You might think one television in your igloo is enough, but some penguins plaster them all over their igloos or stack one on top of another until the whole room is filled up. Sometimes they tune them all to the same channel, and sometimes not!

Sports Fanatic

Whether it's an igloo loaded with surfboards, wall-to-wall treadmills, or piled high with gym mats, sports enthusiasts know how to take their love of athletics to the extreme!

Dancer's Delight

These penguins never get tired of the lights and action of the Night Club, so they've decided to keep on dancing in their own igloos by adding a dance floor, disco ball, stereo equipment, and more!

Bring the Outdoors In

You don't need a yard in your igloo to enjoy nature. Some penguins decorate their igloos with walls of snow and snowmen to create an indoor winter wonderland. Others go for a summer look and load their igloos with flowers, trees, and beach gear.

HINT

Throw a party in your awesome igloo! Unlock your igloo and invite people over. Play some great music and dance the day away!

Join the Community

Of course, Club Penguin is about much more than just games and coins. It's the penguins who live, play, and work here that make it such a special place.

Becoming part of the community can be as easy as making a buddy or as involved as putting on a play at the Stage. In this section, you'll learn many different ways to get into the action.

You've Got to Have Friends

You're hanging out in the Coffee Shop when suddenly you see the 🙂 icon pop up in the upper left corner of your screen. It's a buddy request! But what exactly does it mean to have a buddy?

When a penguin is on your buddy list, you can see if they're online, visit their igloo, and send them mail. It's a way to make sure you can find a friend again after you meet them.

If you want to ask another penguin to be your buddy, click on them. Then click on the 🙂 icon on the bottom of their player card. You'll be asked if you want to ask that penguin to be your buddy. Choose yes, or no if you've changed your mind. If the other penguin accepts, they will appear on your buddy list.

Click on the 🙂 icon on the toolbar on the bottom of your screen to access your buddy list. A yellow smiley face next to the penguin's name means the penguin is in the same server as you. No matter where your buddy is, you can click on their name to see their player card.

Why did the penguin cross the road?

To meet up with his best buddy!

If you don't want to be buddies anymore, click here.

If your buddy is using bad language or threatening you in any way, you can report him or her to the moderator.

Find out where your buddy is by clicking here. Then go there and say hi!

When you click here, you will go right to your friend's igloo, whether your friend is home or not.

You can send mail to any of your buddies no matter where they are when you click here.

Meet Your Friends Online

You probably have friends or brothers or sisters who love Club Penguin as much as you do. To become buddies with them, you have to find them on Club Penguin. Talk before you go on the computer. First, decide which server you will meet on and then pick a time to meet—maybe after school or before dinner. Once you are in the same place on the island, you can click on one another and become buddies. After that, it will be easy to find one another when you're on Club Penguin!

Say What?

Start chatting with your buddies by typing what you want to say using the toolbar on the bottom of your screen. Click on the 💬 icon, and the words will appear in a speech bubble above your head.

If this doesn't work for you, it means you are set up for Ultimate Safe Chat mode. Luckily, there is still a way to communicate with other penguins. You can say hello or good-bye or answer commonly asked questions using the messages option on your toolbar. To access these messages, click on the speech bubble all the way on the left of your toolbar. Then scroll up and over to see all the different choices. Click on the word or phrase you want to say.

You can have as many as one hundred buddies! Once your buddy list is full, you'll need to delete some buddies before you can add more. Remember, friendships on Club Penguin are about quality, not quantity!

DID YOU KNOW?

205

I Feel 😊!

When words can't express how you feel, say it with emotes! These little icons can show how you feel (😠) or help you ask for what you want (🍕). To access them, click on the winking smiley face on the left side of your toolbar. Then scroll up until you see the emote icon that you want, and click on it. It will appear in a speech bubble above your head.

I've found that emotes really come in handy when I'm spending time with my good friends. In fact, I enjoy using them so much that I've discovered five secret emote shortcuts that do not appear on the official Club Penguin list. They are: **E** + **I** = 🐚; **E** + **P** = 🐡; **E** + **M** = 🪙; **E** + **N** = 🌙. Hit **E** + **T** to get 🎵 — with an extra sound! Try it and see what happens.

AUNT ARCTIC SAYS

If scrolling takes too long, you can use these keyboard shortcuts to choose an emote. Just hit the keys to make the emote appear:

e1 = Laughing face

e2 = Smiley

e3 = Straight face

e4 = Frown

e5 = Surprise

e6 = Sticking out tongue

e7 = Wink

e8 = Green sick face

e9 = Red angry face

e0 = Sad face

eu = Crooked face

ec = Coffee cup

eg = Game

eo = Popcorn

ez = Pizza

eq = Ice cream

ek = Cake

el = Good luck

eb = Lightbulb

eh = Heart

ef = Flower

The Newspaper Needs You!

Every Thursday, a new issue of *The Club Penguin Times* hits the stands. Penguins everywhere get the scoop on the latest happenings, get ideas for things to do with their buddies, and learn secrets.

Penguins just like you contribute to the newspaper, too. You can submit:

• original jokes and riddles
• original poetry
• questions for Aunt Arctic

Look in the back of the newspaper to find out how to send in your submissions.

As editor in chief for *The Club Penguin Times* and writer for the "Ask Aunt Arctic" advice column, I am often asked by penguins how they can get their work into the newspaper. I get so many wonderful submissions each week, it's hard to decide what to publish. The number one piece of advice I can offer is be original! I am always looking for something interesting and new.

AUNT ARCTIC SAYS

What's black and white and red all over? A penguin with a sunburn!

Meet Aunt Arctic

Occupation: Aunt Arctic is the advice columnist and editor in chief of *The Club Penguin Times*. Each week she answers two questions in her "Ask Aunt Arctic" column. She loves keeping up on all the happenings on the island, which is why she's perfect for giving tips and secrets.

What You Might Be Surprised to Learn: If a reader asks Aunt Arctic a question and she's not sure of the answer, she'll find out—no matter what! If a penguin wants to know if you can make it to the end of every level of *Jet Pack Adventure* on one tank of fuel, she'll strap on a jet pack and find out.

What She Can't Live Without: Her puffles, of course!

Is It Possible to Meet Aunt Arctic?: Aunt Arctic is very busy with her writing and hadn't been seen much until the Penguin Play Awards. She had such a great time that she now makes special appearances at other events, too.

Favorite Color: Green.

She's Got Friends in High Places: When Aunt Arctic is looking for answers for her column, she's got a lot of friends to turn to. She always seems to know a mini-game expert or the penguins who are planning the latest parties. She's also known to chat with Gary the Gadget Guy.

Would you like to hear a secret about *me*? The next time you read the newspaper, try moving your mouse over my eyeglasses. Something *shady* just might happen . . .

AUNT ARCTIC SAYS

What Will You Play Today?

Now that you know how to make buddies and chat with them, what will you do next? In addition to playing games like *Find Four* and *Sled Racing*, you can act things out with your friends. What do you want to be today: A chef? A knight? A security guard? A wizard? It's up to you!

Something's cooking: One of the most popular activities on the island takes place in the Pizza Parlor. Penguins play waiters, chefs, managers, and customers. But sometimes there's trouble in the Pizza Parlor . . .

Security: Every once in a while penguins act like thieves who try to rob the Pizza Parlor! But it's okay—because other penguins pretend to be police officers and security guards to put a stop to them.

Forest Fun: The Forest is a popular place for penguins to pretend they are different kinds of animals. It's also a place that penguins like to dress up as knights, princesses, wizards, and dragons, and play.

Monster Madness: Especially around Halloween, you'll find lots of penguins pretending to be vampires, zombies, and other spooky creatures.

There are lots of different ways penguins can play. You and your buddies can join any games you see going on, or you can come up with a new one of your own.

Club Penguin Parties

About once a month, Club Penguin throws an official island-wide party. These are celebrations you definitely don't want to miss!

Special decorations are set up all around the island and there's usually lots of new stuff to explore and play with. Free items are almost always given away, too.

What's a rabbit's favorite party game?

Musical *hares*!

Scavenger Hunt!

From time to time, Club Penguin holds special scavenger hunts. Penguins are given clues that lead to the discovery of treasures or new places. The most popular scavenger hunt is the annual Halloween Scavenger Hunt.

Club Penguin's Biggest Bashes!

The Fair: The very first Fair was one of the most exciting parties ever to happen on Club Penguin, thanks to Captain Rockhopper. The pirate brought six new games to play at the party, including *Puffle Shuffle* and *Ring the Bell* (a test of strength). Penguins played games to earn tickets, and then traded in those tickets for cool prizes. It was so much fun that it's returned every year!

Festival of Flight: When the windows in the Underground Pool needed to be fixed, Gary the Gadget Guy had to lift Club Penguin out of the water to do it. Penguins were able to explore the island as it was lifted high into the sky. A hot air balloon ride was offered to the tallest mountain on Club Penguin. Free jet packs were given out, and penguins got to play with the Cloud Maker 3000, creating special clouds for other penguins to admire when they looked through the telescope at the Beacon.

Adventure Party: This party turned the island into an exotic jungle just begging to be explored. Tree houses and waterfalls popped up in the Forest. The ice in the Ice Rink melted and became a blue lagoon for penguins to splash around in. Penguins looking for adventure could don a free safari hat and begin their journey with an exciting Scavenger Hunt.

Puffle Party: When penguins throw a party to celebrate their best friends—puffles—they go all out! The island was turned into a puffle paradise, complete with a ball pit in the Forest for penguins and puffles to jump in and a puffle feeding area where penguins could toss O-berries into the open mouths of hungry puffles. The pool was replaced by an awesome skate-park. Colorful puffle balloons decorated the entire island. It's a party that penguins and their puffles won't soon forget!

Free Items

What's cool on Club Penguin depends on your own personal style and what's happening around the island. Some penguins like accessories to match the theme of the latest party. Others raid the *Costume Trunk* of the current play to dress up in an outrageous costume. Sometimes the latest free item is all the rage. Free items are usually given away at official Club Penguin parties. Here are some items that have always been pretty popular with penguins:

 Propeller cap: You'll often see penguins wearing this flying fashion accessory. If you dance while wearing this item, you will hover in the air!

 Jet pack: This item was available to penguins with a membership at the Festival of Flight. Wear it and then dance to hover in midair.

 Marshmallow stick: Gather around the campfire at the Cove and toast some of these gooey goodies with your friends.

HINT

If you missed getting a free item, don't be sad. Sometimes they're offered again when the next party rolls around. So make sure you read the newspaper to find out when the next party is coming!

Boom box: Penguins who love to bust a move carry these around.

 Lollipop: Have a sweet tooth? This sweet treat will do the trick!

 Wizard hat: Abracadabra! This hat is fashion magic—and great for role-playing, too.

Water wings: Ready for a swim? Dance while wearing this item and you'll paddle through the water.

 Pumpkin antennae: Penguins were able to go trick-or-treating in style with this Halloween freebie.

Club Penguin Needs You!

Want to pitch in and help make Club Penguin a fun place for everyone who visits? Here's a look at some cool things penguins have done—and things you can do right now!

Contribute to *The Club Penguin Times* and the Art Gallery: Submit jokes, poetry, and comic strips to the newspaper. Go to the Book Room to find out how you can submit your artwork for display at the art gallery!

Enter Contests: From time to time, you'll have the chance to share your special talents by entering contests in the fields of ice sculpture, art, writing, igloo decorating, and more.

Take the Penguin Poll: Share your opinions about Club Penguin by clicking on "Community" on the home page and answering the latest poll question.

Be a Tour Guide: Help new penguins out by showing them around the island. (See page 21 for more info.)

Be a Secret Agent: Keep Club Penguin safe by going on missions and reporting penguins who are behaving badly to the moderator. (See page 178 for more info.)

There's always something new and exciting going on. Make sure to read *The Club Penguin Times* every week or check the "What's New" blog to find out the latest activities. You can find it on the top left part of your screen.

Even More Penguin Fun!

Your Club Penguin experience doesn't have to end when you log off. There are lots of cool things you can do right from the Club Penguin home page, clubpenguin.com. Click on the orange penguin or "Community" to access these things to do:

Penguins Around the World: Check out photos from fans just like you and submit your own photos.

Make Some Art: Click on "Activities" to print out coloring pages, and pages that show you how to draw penguins yourself. You'll also find arts and crafts projects with instructions on how to make a diorama, a ninja flip-book, and more!

Get a Laugh: Click on "Comics" to read Club Penguin comic strips you won't find anywhere else!

Cook Up Some Fun: Click on "Activities" to get yummy recipes you can make with the help of an adult!

Penguin-ize Your Computer: Click on "Wallpaper" to download wallpaper for your computer featuring your favorite games, Captain Rockhopper, and more!

Penguin Pride: Do you have your own website or blog? Click on "Banners" to download banners with the Club Penguin logo. Show the world that you love Club Penguin!

Outdoor Adventures: Take your love of Club Penguin outside by clicking on "Activities" and then "Outdoor Activities."

What does a clam do at a Club Penguin party?

He *shell*abrates!

How Do I Do That?

If you have a question, asking a Tour Guide is a good way to get an answer. You could also ask a buddy for help, or write to Aunt Arctic in *The Club Penguin Times*. Right now, you can check out the next few pages for answers to some of the most commonly asked questions.

How Do I Pour Coffee?
Or Play Guitar?
Or Do All Those Other Cool
Things I See Penguins Doing?

It's not as hard as you think. There's a simple formula for most special actions:

special item + dance (or wave) = special action

First, you need a special item. Put it on. Don't wear anything else. Then dance or wave to set the special action in motion.

Here are a few examples of how the special formula works. Of course, the best way to find out how to do a special action is to experiment and see what works!

electric guitar + dance = play guitar

jackhammer + dance = drill

propeller cap + dance = hover

whistle + wave = blow whistle

How Do I Find the Hidden Pins?

Every two weeks, a new pin is hidden on Club Penguin. A pin is a small picture that you can add to your player card. To learn when a new pin is out, check the last page of the newspaper.

Searching for a pin is fun. Check all over Club Penguin, and look for a small icon that doesn't belong.

There are two things you should know when searching for pins. First, a pin is never hidden in town because town is too crowded. And a pin will never be hidden in the same place two times in a row.

Cool Pins!

There have been more than fifty pins released since Club Penguin opened. Here is a sampling of them. You can also search through the yearbooks on the shelf in the Book Room to find some more hidden pieces of the past.

All About You

This tour might be over, but you can have new adventures on Club Penguin every day. Take this fun quiz, then use the pages in this section to keep a record of your experience.

Which Penguin Character Are You Most Like?

Which Club Penguin character are you most like: Captain Rockhopper, Aunt Arctic, Cadence, Gary the Gadget Guy, or Sensei? To find out, take this quiz. Pick the best answer to each question. Then add up the points you get for each answer. Use the chart at the end to learn your penguin identity.

1. What do you do when you're bored?
   a. Turn on the music and try out the latest dance move (5 pts.)
   b. You're never bored! Life is an adventure! (4 pts.)
   c. Take apart your clock radio to see how it works (3 pts.)
   d. Read a book (2 pts.)
   e. Put on your *gi*, or karate clothing, and do some martial arts training (1 pt.)

2. Where is your favorite place to visit?
   a. Night Club (5 pts.)
   b. Lighthouse (4 pts.)
   c. Secret Agent HQ (3 pts.)
   d. Book Room (2 pts.)
   e. Dojo (1 pt.)

3. When you reach for a snack, what do you grab?
   a. Water. You need to rehydrate after all that dancing (5 pts.)
   b. Cream soda (4 pts.)
   c. Pizza with anchovies (3 pts.)
   d. You give a snack to your puffles instead (2 pts.)
   e. Fortune cookies (1 pt.)

4. What's your favorite item of clothing?
   a. Anything, as long as it's colorful! (5 pts.)
   b. A sturdy pair of black boots with shiny buckles (4 pts.)
   c. Your white lab coat (3 pts.)
   d. A comfy sweater to keep you warm (2 pts.)
   e. Your martial arts belt (1 pt.)

5. How would your friends describe you?
   a. Fun-loving and popular (5 pts.)
   b. Loud, adventurous, and fun to be around (4 pts.)
   c. Smart and curious (3 pts.)
   d. Kind and helpful (2 pts.)
   e. Wise beyond your years (1 pt.)

Add Up Your Score:

22-25 points:

You are Cadence!

You are the penguin who's always starting parties. You're happiest when you're with your friends dancing, joking, and having fun. You love music and are a great dancer. You love meeting new people and are happy to show them how to become a great dancer, too.

18-21 points:

You are Captain Rockhopper!

You are a brave penguin who is always ready for adventure. Whenever there's a new party on Club Penguin, you make sure to explore every corner of the island to make sure you're not missing anything. You love water and enjoy swimming and water sports. You'd make a great lifeguard!

13-17 points:
You are Gary the Gadget Guy!

If there is a problem to be solved, you are the penguin who tries to fix it. You love science and would love to work in a lab some day. Whenever a free item comes out, you are one of the first penguins to try it to see how it works. You enjoy helping out when Club Penguin has work parties to fix or build things around the island.

9-12 points:
You are Aunt Arctic!

You love to read. You're also a very helpful penguin and probably enjoy being a Tour Guide. When you see new penguins who are confused you talk to them and try to set them in the right direction. When you're not reading, writing, or helping others, you love taking care of your puffles!

5-8 points:
You are Sensei!

You are a thoughtful penguin who enjoys the discipline of martial arts training. You probably already have your black belt in *Card-Jitsu* by now—if not, start training! You'll be great. You may be wise beyond your years, but like Sensei, you know that a ninja's training never stops.

The Basics

My penguin's name: _____

Favorite penguin color:_____

My puffles:

Name   Color

_____   _____

_____   _____

_____   _____

_____   _____

_____   _____

_____   _____

_____   _____

My best buddies:

_____

_____

_____

_____

_____

_____

_____

_____

Favorites

Favorite game: _____

Favorite hangout: _____

Favorite party spot: _____

Favorite clothing item: _____

Favorite furniture item:_____

Favorite book in the Library: _____

Favorite Club Penguin character: _____

Favorite Club Penguin party: _____

Favorite pizza: _____

Draw your penguin here:

Highest Game Scores

Aqua Grabber

Score: _____   Date: _____
Score: _____   Date: _____
Score: _____   Date: _____

Astro-Barrier

Score: _____   Date: _____
Score: _____   Date: _____
Score: _____   Date: _____

Bean Counters

Score: _____   Date: _____
Score: _____   Date: _____
Score: _____   Date: _____

Cart Surfer

Score: _____   Date: _____
Score: _____   Date: _____
Score: _____   Date: _____

Catchin' Waves

Score: _____   Date: _____
Score: _____   Date: _____
Score: _____   Date: _____

Dance Contest

Score: _____   Date: _____
Score: _____   Date: _____
Score: _____   Date: _____

DJ3K

Score: _____   Date: _____
Score: _____   Date: _____
Score: _____   Date: _____

Hydro-Hopper

Score: _____ Date: _____

Score: _____ Date: _____

Score: _____ Date: _____

Ice Fishing

Score: _____ Date: _____

Score: _____ Date: _____

Score: _____ Date: _____

Jet Pack Adventure

Score: _____ Date: _____

Score: _____ Date: _____

Score: _____ Date: _____

Mancala

Score: _____ Date: _____

Score: _____ Date: _____

Score: _____ Date: _____

Pizzatron 3000

Score: _____ Date: _____

Score: _____ Date: _____

Score: _____ Date: _____

Puffle Roundup

Score: _____ Date: _____

Score: _____ Date: _____

Score: _____ Date: _____

Thin Ice

Score: _____ Date: _____

Score: _____ Date: _____

Score: _____ Date: _____

Free Items

Item: _____ Date: _____

Item: _____ Date: _____

Item: _____ Date: _____

Item: _____ Date: _____

Item: _____ Date: _____

Item: _____ Date: _____

Item: _____ Date: _____

Item: _____ Date: _____

Item: _____ Date: _____

Item: _____ Date: _____

Item: _____ Date: _____

Item: _____ Date: _____

Item: _____ Date: _____

Item: _____ Date: _____

Item: _____ Date: _____

Item: _____ Date: _____

Item: _____ Date: _____

Index